ENDORSEMENTS

Joan Hunter has ministered with us often and I have been an eyewitness to the many miracles that God works under her hands. One of the things I love about Joan is that she truly lives everything she preaches. Her heart is to see the entire Body walk in wholeness and move into the fullness of healing ministry. Joan ministers healing not only to the physical body, but also to the heart issues that are often the root. You will love *Healing Starts Now! Expanded Edition.* It will give you keys for receiving healing and tools to help others come into wholeness. This is a must read!

Patricia King
Founder of XPmedia
XPmedia.com

To know Dr. Joan Hunter is to love her. She is one of the most gifted healers of this age. She exudes the love and light of God. She carries a double portion of the healing mantle with a great grace and authority. Because of her vast scriptural knowledge and spiritual experiences on the topic of healing, she is able to compile this amazing manual called *Healing Starts Now! Expanded Edition.* In these pages you will find the keys to unlock your own healing and the healing of others. Joan shares her practical skills and healing techniques that will enable every believer to relate these healing applications in their own lives. In these pages Joan goes into great depth to remove the mystery, making healing appear simple and matter-of-fact. Jesus' commission was to go into the world, preach the Gospel, make disciples, heal the sick, cast out devils, and raise the dead. If you have a desire to walk out your own commission in the healing ministry, this training manual, *Healing Starts Now! Expanded Edition*, is a must.

Dr. Barbie L. Breathitt Ph.D.
Breath of the Spirit Ministries, Inc.
Author of *DREAM ENCOUNTERS*,
Seeing Your Destiny from God's Perspective
www.BarbieBreathitt.com
www.MyOnar.com

Dr. Joan Hunter is one of the most humble Christians I have ever met. She has exercised her faith for over 30 years, never wavering, strengthening her spiritual muscles to a degree many Christians only dream about. The Lord is using Joan for His glory as she lays hands on thousands who are sick and they do recover, in Jesus' name!

Healing Starts Now! Expanded Edition imparts great faith while teaching practical application that is tried and true. This power-packed manual will help you live a supernatural life, naturally.

Joan often comments that if she can do it, you can do it! She means that and so does Jesus. It's time to take the demonstration of the power of the Gospel to the "4 corners" of the earth. I highly recommend this manual to all who need healing or know someone who does…and that would be everybody.

Paulette Reed
Founder & President
Prophetic Arrow Ministries

Our friend Joan Hunter is among the most notable Christian ministers in our day whom God is using around the world to heal the sick and to train believers to do the same. In this comprehensive, illustrated healing manual, *Healing Starts Now! Expanded Edition*, she demystifies, and makes so practical, how to pray for and see immediate, amazing results in healing and the miraculous! She is an authentic, anointed woman of God who is naturally supernatural and a joy to be with. We recommend that every believer make this manual a valuable weapon in their arsenal to destroy the works of darkness and to glorify God by doing the works of Jesus!

Jim & Ramona Rickard, Founders
Resurrection Apostolic International Network &
The International Association of Healing Ministries

This book is one of the most practical manuals on the ministry of healing. Joan combines extensive experience, medical insights, and biblical revelation, and places it all in a down-to-earth format that will benefit every believer.

Eli Hendricks, Senior Pastor
LifeWay Community Church, Tallahassee, Florida

HEALING STARTS
STARTS
Now!

EXPANDED EDITION

HEALING STARTS Now!

EXPANDED EDITION

COMPLETE
TRAINING MANUAL

Joan Hunter

DESTINY IMAGE® PUBLISHERS, INC.

P.O. Box 310, Shippensburg, PA 17257-0310

"Promoting Inspired Lives."

This book and all other Destiny Image, Revival Press, MercyPlace, Fresh Bread, Destiny Image Fiction, and Treasure House books are available at Christian bookstores and distributors worldwide.

For a U.S. bookstore nearest you, call 1-800-722-6774.

For more information on foreign distributors, call 717-532-3040.

Reach us on the Internet: www.destinyimage.com.

ISBN 13 Trade Paper: 978-0-7684-4223-6

ISBN 13 Ebook: 978-0-7684-8549-3

For Worldwide Distribution, Printed in the U.S.A.

6 / 17

DEDICATION

It is with joy, admiration, and loving memory that I dedicate this book to my parents, Charles and Frances Hunter.

During the 1970s and 1980s they helped restore the ministry of healing to the forefront by presenting a powerful and effective model of healing to the Church. Millions were saved, healed, and filled with the Spirit in 49 foreign countries and throughout the United States.

They were pioneers in demonstrating God's healing power.

They influenced a generation of Christian leaders and taught hundreds of thousands that "if Charles and Frances Hunter can do it...you can do it, too!"

Charles and Frances Hunter broke the paradigm of the "singled out anointed healing minister" that had dominated the thinking of the Church up until that time.

Healing is not only the children's bread, it also is the work of all God's people, not just a few individuals.

This manual is an extension of their lives and all I learned from them, plus all that God has taught me over the years while serving them and Him.

Now in the 21st century God is once again raising up the ministry of healing to empower the Church and save the lost. I believe this manual will play an important role in equipping the Church to heal the sick and show His power, that many will want to know Him.

To millions around the world they were Charles and Frances Hunter or "The Happy Hunters." To me they were Mom and Dad.

They will always be simply remembered, they will always be loved, and they will always be missed.

I am blessed to be a blessing, and so are you!

Acknowledgments

Many years ago God gave me a dream to empower the Church to minister healing both within the Body of Christ and to the lost because many will not believe unless they first see. It is my belief that God is once again raising up the neglected *ministry* of healing within the Church around the world, just like the ministry of intercession, as a means to demonstrate His love, save the lost, and glorify His name. The Noris have made a committment to the ministry of healing, both within Destiny Image and by helping me publish this manual. I believe this manual will become a landmark in the ministry of healing for decades to come because, to my knowledge, no one else has ever published such a clear, concise, and comprehensive approach to the *ministry* of healing.

I have done everything I can to make the ministry of healing practical and simple enough that anyone can do it. I have tried to take the bizarre and mysterious elements out of the ministry of healing and put the tools I have gained after more than 30 years of praying for the sick, in your hands. I know what you are about to read really works because I have used these prayers successfully thousands of times and trained others to do the same. Thanks to everyone at Destiny Image for helping me publish this book.

I also want to say thanks to my editor/assistant writer, Naida Johnson Trott. For many years she faithfully served my parents and now she serves me in the same role. Naida, this manual is a better resource work for the Church because of your participation in its development. Thank you.

A special thank you to:

Spice Lussier, NMD, for her help and advice in *Healing Starts Now!* Especially the chapter she wrote, entitled "Nurture the Natural Man"(www.inspiremedicine.com). Kelley Murrell, for his expertise on editing and proofing.

Susan, Tracy (for keeping me on a time line) and many others who helped put this project together.

I also would like to thank those who contributed to this book in so many other ways—the hundreds of believers who have learned and applied the principles of the teachings, as well as those who have contributed information from their experiences in the area of healing, and finally, those who have been set free as I have used the revelations that God has given me to use on them.

That the God of our Lord Jesus Christ, the Father of glory, may give to you the spirit of wisdom and revelation in the knowledge of Him, the eyes of your understanding being enlightened; that you may know what is the hope of His calling, what are the riches of the glory of His inheritance in the saints, and what is the exceeding greatness of His power toward us who believe, according to the working of His mighty power (Ephesians 1:17-19).

CONTENTS

PART I
HEALING

PART II
THE ROOT CAUSES OF DISEASES

PREFACE

Joan Hunter knows that you don't have to be in full-time ministry or to be a spiritual giant to pray for the sick. Her faith to heal body, soul, and spirit was forged in the furnace.

How does God minister through a woman who was so badly abused and betrayed, whose father left before she was born, who was abused by uncles, abused by a husband, diagnosed with breast cancer, left with nothing? How did He choose a woman who in elementary school was told she was retarded and would never amount to anything? How did God take that person and raise her up to be an evangelist? She is that person!

The former things no longer come to mind in Joan Hunter's life. She desires every believer to be set free from the bondages of the past and to walk and minister in newness of life.

This is a great moment in your life as a Christian. You are about to discover just how effective an ambassador of God's love you can be. Many believers are frustrated by a feeling of helplessness in the face of a world that is indifferent to the things of God. Others feel disconnected from the supernatural Christianity described in the Gospels and the Book of Acts.

However, you now hold in your hands a practical guide for accessing the power of God on behalf of all people, Christians and non-Christians alike. There is no more powerful demonstration of God's love for the lost than to heal their bodies. God can do what doctors cannot do, and He will use you to demonstrate His love if you choose to cooperate with Him. Once you lay hold of these principles, you will have more confidence in sharing your faith with the lost than ever before.

God can and will use you to heal the sick wherever you go. You, too, will lay hands on the sick, and they will recover (see Mark 16:17-18).

Susan Wittman

PART I

HEALING

secrets has sent archeologists to isolated areas of the world to dig through layers and layers of accumulated silt and dirt to unearth the smallest particles of ancient cultures. Ways to "heal" the sick have always been of great interest. Every culture has placed great emphasis on the "healing arts." The medicine man or woman was always highly respected and revered because of his or her "secrets" to prolonging life or to healing mysterious symptoms.

Healing is not a new subject, but the emphasis through the centuries has been primarily on the physical body. Herbs, chemicals, warmth/cold, move/don't move—all were prescribed in one way or another to help man return to normal health. Somewhere through the years, these prescriptions became official medications and medical treatments. The person prescribing these "cures" became the "doctor" or "physician."

Today, we say doctors "practice medicine," and that sounds strange, but it is true. There is not one way to cure any disease. Doctors prescribe the drug or treatment of choice that usually helps the symptoms or identified condition. If it doesn't work, they prescribe another medication or another treatment. Occasionally, two or three options are tried over several weeks or months before an acceptable outcome is achieved.

God has blessed mankind with wise and caring medical personnel to help us make educated choices to preserve and maintain optimal health. I will never discount their importance or contributions to healing the sick and infirm. However, too often through the centuries, as science has progressed, man put his faith in logic and scientific principles rather than in the ultimate Healer. Mankind chose to find truth within himself and forgot his Creator.

Although medical practitioners of every hue have worked tirelessly to heal every area of human suffering, they have failed miserably. There are many medical choices to heal the body and mind, but few that accomplish true healing and none that bring creative restoration. When they reach an impasse in their diagnoses and lack of treatment, medical advice becomes, "Live with it," "It is in your mind," or "Go home and set your affairs in order!"

From the moment of birth, whenever babies feel uncomfortable, they "cry" for help, for "relief": "Fix me." "Make me feel better." Essentially, we never stop searching for an answer for the aches and pains of aging, the cramps or muscle spasms from exercise, the bumps and scrapes from falls or sports injuries, the allergies or cold symptoms as the seasons pass, or a stomachache from eating the wrong foods. We all want to be comfortable and free from pain.

The World's Answer Is Expensive

Millions of dollars are spent yearly on health insurance. Thousands of sick people are admitted and discharged from hospitals daily in their search for optimal health. They agree to surgery to fix this or medications to fix that. Slowly but surely the insurance industry has taken such control of society that the uninsured are almost second-class citizens. They are unprotected, gambling with their lives, destroyed by a simple illness, or forced to remain trapped in a job they don't enjoy just to maintain their insurance coverage. Even hospitalization for illness or birth of a child can be out of reach without "proof" of insurance for payment of basic medical services. We have heard of people dying in emergency rooms of county hospitals "waiting" in endless lines for "free" medical assistance. People around the world search endlessly for "relief" from their medical problems.

Credit companies are raking in the profits because people think they need to buy on credit for instant gratification. Paying cash for anything is fast becoming the oddity instead of the norm. Buying one more thing, eating at one more fancy restaurant, impressing one more friend or business associate seems to be the ultimate answer to making it in this complicated world. Fighting the corporate battle, sealing just one more deal, being introduced to the next powerful person will surely open the door to success.

Once success is achieved, the fear of losing it all sets in. The merry-go-round of worry, pills, drinking, and partying starts its cycle and stress rears its ugly head in the midst of dysfunctional families, problem children, and divorce. As life spins out of control, the search for peace and healing becomes more intense, more desperate. Physical, mental, and emotional problems add their pressure and the answers seem further and further out of reach.

God waits patiently for His children to finally fall to their knees and call out to Him for His divine intervention. Even with His miracles, man often explains them away and discounts their existence. However, through the ages a faithful few tenaciously hung on to His promises. These few kept the Word of God alive in spite of the teachings of the Church to the contrary; the few who had been miraculously healed would not keep silent. Those few knew Jesus lived within them and was the same yesterday, today, and tomorrow…the Healer (see Heb. 13:8).

The faithful believers were always there; however, they often still suffered from illness and infirmities. Where did illness come from? The Garden of Eden was pure and free from sin. There was no illness, no infirmity. What happened?

We all know the story of Adam and Eve. When disobedience entered, it also opened the door for sin. When God's ultimate protection was removed, sin opened the door to illness and disease. Man chose to leave the peaceful existence communing with God to go his "own way" in the world. Eve had her input in the situation, but Adam had been given the ultimate responsibility. God will not interfere with man's will.

In modern times, faith in the healing power of God has been minimized. Yes, it happened in Bible times, but not today, some say. However, God hasn't changed. Jesus hasn't changed. The gifts God gave as recorded in Scripture are still ours today. Jesus did it all many years ago. He paid the price. Why don't people believe today?

Perhaps a lack of knowledge based on misplaced beliefs from parents or mentors, misconceptions, man's religious beliefs, scientific explanations, or anger at God for previous personal losses or illnesses have blinded man's eyes to the truth. How often man reads the Bible without hearing the Truth of His Word. Ask God to open your eyes to His perfect Truth right now.

Jesus Is the Answer

The number one answer for all our problems is Jesus. He is the one Source of all healing for all diseases, discomfort, or pain. He is the only "second opinion" anyone ever needs to look for or request. He knows how to cure all conditions, no matter how small or large, how simple or complicated. He is the Answer.

He is the Physician, He is the Counselor, and He is the Provider. He knows the root causes of our infirmities and ailments. His healing power is not limited to physical or mental conditions. He can heal the heart and soul of any person. He heals all aspects of our being...the mental, physical, emotional, and financial.

Why am I explaining healing to you? Most people consider it to be a complicated subject, a mysterious unknown entity with impossible answers hidden and unattainable. If you depend on science, medicine, or theology for your total recovery, healing can be a very long and complicated journey.

However, if you recognize the one Person who has all the answers to any disease you have, the answer is simple. His name is Jesus. In concert with our Heavenly Father and His Holy Spirit, anyone can be healed. Jesus can heal the whole man.

Does it take a long time? NO. However, occasionally the manifestation of a healing does take some time. Is healing guaranteed? No, I can't promise or guarantee anything. Only God heals. However, after dozens of years ministering around the world in various countries, I can share endless experiences of healings that I have witnessed personally as well as documented testimonies of healings that occurred during healing schools.

If you put the principles contained in this book into practice, you, too, can be healed and whole!

CHAPTER TWO

OUR AUTHORITY IN CHRIST

...in Him we live and move and have our being...
(Acts 17:28).

All Authority Belongs to God

Few Christians will argue about God's ultimate authority. Those who believe in God's existence, His omniscience, His omnipresence, and His omnipotence know their Creator is the God of Abraham, Isaac, and Jacob. In other words, our Creator is the God of the Holy Bible. No one, nothing, in fact, not even the angels in Heaven can refute or supersede God's ultimate authority over everyone and everything. Through Jesus, God is the Author and Finisher of our faith (see Heb. 12:2). Through Him, *"we live and move and have our being"* (Acts 17:28).

Some believe their lives are dependent on fate, genes, or the food they eat. Although some of these things do affect us, this mindset allows no place for God. The common practice is to depend on science and medical doctors, and they do have a God-given place.

As Christians, we can receive a new life, a new way of thinking, and a new way to walk in health. By accepting, be-lieving, and walking in His wisdom and footsteps, we can live in divine health and minister healing to others. Think of one hand reaching up to connect to God's supernatural power while the other hand reaches out to connect to the hurting, the sick, and the oppressed. We are simply the conduit between God and the person to whom we are ministering.

Our primary responsibility as given in the Great Commission is to spread the Good News. Some receive their salvation easily. Perhaps you did. However, in a "show me" world, signs, wonders, and miracles often draw the skeptical into His fellowship quicker than other evangelical methods.

What makes me, an average person, believe I can minister healing to others? Without Jesus, I cannot do a thing. However, with His authority, I can see the sick recover and I can also cast out demons. I can set the captives free. I can be a conduit of love directly from the Father to the world. Are you ready to participate in this incredible experience?

Can anyone lay hands on the sick? No. There are some requirements. First, you must be a believer in Jesus Christ. He must be living in your heart. As He changes your heart and mind, you want to, in fact, you are almost compelled to share His Good News with others. As you study to show yourself approved (see 2 Tim. 2:15), His Truth invades every area of your being. Suddenly, you realize Jesus works through you to touch others not only for salvation but also for healing of their body, mind, and soul. You will say, "I never knew healing could be so easy!"

Praying for healing can be as simple as saying, "Be healed!" Some believe just speaking positive words over a situation will bring results. Those words, too, may help. However, when I want results, I go directly to the Source. I want to see a miracle when I pray. What do I say? What words do I use? What have I learned about praying for the sick? Open up your mind and heart to the principles contained in this manual.

Father, let me be open and receptive to all You have for me. I want to reach out and connect with others. I want more and more people to be saved, set free, and healed. Thank You for Jesus' sacrifice, which allows us to appropriate His mind, heart, and wisdom. Let me be sensitive to His Holy Spirit and respond each and every time You want me to pray for healing both for others and for myself. Amen.

When I pray for healing, I pray in the name and in the authority of the great Physician—Jesus Christ. **His authority is my foundation to pray for the healing of myself and others.** I have taught thousands to do the same. Do you understand God's authority?

Even Nebuchadnezzar, a powerful, idol-worshiping pagan king, came to understand the King of kings' supreme authority and that God can do whatever He wants:

...He does according to His will in the army of heaven and among the inhabitants of the earth. No one can restrain His hand or say to Him, "What have You done?" (Daniel 4:35)

In the New Testament, Jesus called His disciples together to teach them to follow in His footsteps. In order to increase His influence, Jesus had to multiply Himself through His disciples and other followers. Time after time, He showed by example who He was and what He could do. He proved He was the Son of God and walked in His Father's authority.

Even though they had already seen Him work miracles, Jesus' disciples said with awe, *"Who can this be, that even the winds and the sea obey Him?"* (Matt. 8:27). In the same chapter of Matthew, a Roman centurion recognized Jesus' authority because of his own experience as a military commander *"under authority"* (Matt. 8:9). He had such great faith in Jesus' authority that he asked Him simply to speak the word and his servant would be healed.

But the officer said, "Lord, I am not worthy to have You come into my home. Just say the word from where You are, and my

servant will be healed. I know this because I am under the authority of my superior officers, and I have authority over my soldiers. I only need to say, 'Go,' and they go, or 'Come,' and they come. And if I say to my slaves, 'Do this,' they do it." When Jesus heard this, He was amazed. Turning to those who were following Him, He said, "I tell you the truth, I haven't seen faith like this in all Israel!" (Matthew 8:8-10 NLT)

Jesus did what His Father told Him to do as well as when to do it (see John 5:19). Just like Jesus, we are to believe and walk in faith that God is able to subdue all things—including all diseases. Every name (thing, disease, demon, or situation) has to bow at the name of Jesus (see Phil. 2:9-11). Knowing that, how can we doubt divine healing as Jesus works through you and I, His disciples of today? Paul wrote to the church at Philippi:

He will take our weak mortal bodies and change them into glorious bodies like His own, using the same power with which He will bring everything under His control (Philippians 3:21 NLT).

A foundational scriptural prayer that reveals a greater understanding of Jesus and His authority is Paul's prayer to the Ephesians:

That the God of our Lord Jesus Christ, the Father of glory, may give to you the spirit of wisdom and revelation in the knowledge of Him, the eyes of your understanding being enlightened; that you may know what is the hope of His calling, what are the riches of the glory of His inheritance in the saints, and what is the exceeding greatness of His power toward us who believe, according to the working of His mighty power (Ephesians 1:17-19).

His Authority Over Sickness

There is no question that Jesus' authority over all things includes sickness. Those who have received Christ as Lord and

Savior have been set free from sin and death and, according to Ephesians 1:20, are raised up together and seated with Him in heavenly places. Jesus has commanded us to serve Him and to heal others from that position of authority: *"All authority has been given to Me in heaven and on earth. Go therefore..."* (Matt. 28:18-19). He also said that miraculous signs would follow those who believe—one of those signs is that, as a believer, you will lay hands on the sick and they will recover. Jesus said:

> *...Go into all the world and preach the gospel to every creature. He who believes and is baptized will be saved; but he who does not believe will be condemned. And these signs will follow those who believe: In My name they will cast out demons; they will speak with new tongues; they will take up serpents; and if they drink anything deadly, it will by no means hurt them; they will lay hands on the sick, and they will recover* (Mark 16:15-18).

When Jesus ministered to people, He healed *all*—not some— of their diseases. *All* means every person was healed of every disease. For example, Matthew 12:15 says, *"great multitudes followed Him, and He healed them all."* Likewise, Luke described how *"...all those who had any that were sick with various diseases brought them to Him; and He laid His hands on every one of them and healed them"* (Luke 4:40). (See also Matthew 4:24; Mark 6:56; Luke 6:19; Acts 5:16.) Only one Scripture indicates that Jesus could not do any mighty works because of unbelief (see Matt. 13:58). Those who came believing received.

As Jesus suffered on the cross, the Father placed our sins, weaknesses, infirmities, and diseases on His body, opening the door for us to walk in total health. Because of the stripes so brutally inflicted on Jesus' back, we have the right to claim our healing.

Who Himself bore our sins in His own body on the tree, that we, having died to sins, might live for righteousness—by whose stripes you were healed (1 Peter 2:24).

Jesus Has Given His Authority to Us

We have read and heard the miraculous things Jesus did during His lifetime, but He was only one person. Even with His supernatural gifts, He was still human. He could not physically be everywhere and touch everyone who had a need. God had a plan. Through Jesus as the perfect sacrifice for our sins, He freed us from the curse of sin and death. Before He returned to Heaven, He instructed His disciples to wait for the Comforter. Through Jesus' death and the Holy Spirit, Jesus lives within every believer. We have His mind, His love, and His healing to draw upon and use in our everyday life.

Most Christians believe that God can heal, but they are not certain that God can heal through them. They have experienced or been taught that healing is reserved only for the chosen few, the elite of the church elders, or after an extended time of fasting and prayer. The Scriptures do not say Jesus went away to fast, pray, and then returned later to lay hands on the sick and saw them recover.

Certainly, I believe in fasting and prayer, but I choose to do exactly what Jesus did. He just reached out and healed the sick. Jesus taught by example. He showed His disciples what to do and then encouraged them to do the same thing using His name.

In Luke 9:1, did Jesus call His disciples together and give them authority to cast out evil spirits and heal *most* diseases? No! He wants to heal *every* sickness—not just some. He told them, *"...I have given you authority over **all** the power of the enemy"* (Luke 10:19a NLT). He purposely instructed them to do mighty works in His name. He empowered His followers to do miracles and speak healing into other people as they traveled and spread the Good News.

Just as Jesus gave that authority to His disciples, He gives it to you today. You must be willing and ready to reach out to others. Using your faith in Him and His Word, you must expect to move in His power to heal. Jesus also wants you healthy and whole. How can you be prepared to do His work and reach others with the Good News of the Gospel if you are sick and restricted to a bed? He wants you ready, willing, and able each and every time He calls.

If you happen to be sick and have not yet experienced total healing, can you still pray for the sick? Most emphatically, YES! A perfect example of this is my Mom, Frances Hunter. From her wheelchair, she prayed for thousands. When Mom and Dad traveled to Russia, four big strong men had to carry her and her wheelchair up flights of stairs to reach a church gathering. She taught on healing, prayed for the sick, laid hands on the sick, and saw them healed by the power of God flowing through her. Then the men carried her down all those stairs to go on to the next meeting. Even when she became bedridden during her final days, she continued to reach out and pray for anyone who was nearby or who called to talk on the phone. Even as weak as she was at that time, God's amazing power flowed through her to heal others.

Are you ready to hear His voice? Do you want to lay hands on the sick and see them recover? Are you willing to do greater works than Jesus did? If you are a believer in the Lord Jesus Christ, you have the ability to do everything Jesus did when He walked on this earth. He told His disciples:...*He who believes in Me, the works that I do he will do also; and greater works then these he will do, because I go to My Father. And whatever you ask in My name, that will I do, that the Father may be glorified in the Son. If you ask anything in My name, I will do it* (John 14:12–14).

You and I are His disciples in today's world. He is giving us the same instructions that He gave His followers. When and where do you start? It is simple. You walk amongst hurting and sick people every day. Listen and be willing to reach out. Be sensitive to God's prompting and to the people around you. Remember, *"we have the mind of Christ"* so *"let this mind be in you which was also in Christ Jesus"* (1 Cor. 2:16; Phil. 2:5).

Everybody you walk by is within three feet of their healing. They do not realize how close they are to a miracle with their name on it. Keep in mind, their healing depends on your decision to obey the leading of the Holy Spirit. Listen, be willing, and act with confidence. You must first extend your hand and ask, "May I pray for you?" When they agree, lay hands on them and pray for whatever they need.

Does God really want you to minister healing? Do you want to be in His perfect will? Many people are searching for God's direction in their lives. For an answer, open up your Bible. His Word tells us what to do: GO… DO…. Lay hands on the sick and see them recover. Just as Jesus knew His authority, you need to know, accept, and speak with the authority given by the King of kings and Lord of lords.

Remember, it is not your *ability* that matters, but your *availability.*

Heal With His Authority

You may think that healing can't possibly be that easy. Why not? Jesus said, *"Ask, and you will receive"* (John 16:24). Many people try to make healing too difficult or too complicated. They believe hours of prayer are necessary before a miracle will happen. Successfully laying hands on the sick and seeing them recover is not a matter of how hard or loud you pray. I just ask God to release His power and people are healed—it is that simple. In fact, some have been healed when I whispered quietly in their ear.

You are all called to lay hands on the sick and see them recover. As you read these instructions, envision yourself walking up to someone and laying your hands on them. Practice talking to the person in your mirror or with your family. Flowery words are not necessary because God hears your heart. Do not hesitate because you cannot remember exactly what I said or how I said it. Let God give you the words to say as you pray. Understand what your gifting is and what you are called to do. Be confident that God has called you to the Kingdom for such a time as this. Envision yourself reaching out, speaking healing, and seeing them recover. Become what you believe.

I know that I walk in God's authority. I do not need to muster up the anointing. I do not have to pray for hours begging God for His anointing. I know that I walk in it whether I am at church, riding on a ferry, flying in an airplane, shopping in a store, or visiting a restroom. No matter where I am or what I am doing, I walk in an anointing that does not depend on anything or anybody but Jesus.

Do not tell people they have to wait to receive their healing until they go to church to hear praise and worship or until "Joan's" next healing meeting in a month or so. Praise and worship is wonderful, and many people have been healed listening to anointed music. Many do get their healing during church or at my meetings, but why make them wait when their healing is as close as you are? You can pray for somebody and see him healed without praise and worship. Do not make healing dependent on the atmosphere. If the atmosphere does not seem right for healing, change it. Speak to the atmosphere and watch it change. If the area is too noisy, ask the person to move to a quiet corner.

Know Jesus is with you. You do not do the healing. He does it through you. A police officer in the middle of a street does not actually have the strength to stop a huge truck by lifting his hands, but he has federal and state laws backing him up. A 200-pound man stops a 10,000- pound truck by raising a hand. Does he peek out from behind a pole and say, "Please, stop your truck"? No, he confidently walks out in the middle of the road, raises his hand, and all the drivers pay attention and follow the police officer's orders.

A friend of mine worked in a protection detail for young princes from another country while they traveled in the United States. Wherever they went, the princes walked with their heads held high, knowing that they could go and do whatever their father directed them to do. They knew who their father was and walked with confidence and self-assurance at all times.

Through Jesus, God has given us His authority. I know who my Father is and I choose to walk in His authority every day. Are you ready to join me?

God's Responsibility

Jesus took stripes on His back so that you and I could be healed of every kind of disease. He entered a town and every sick person He prayed for was healed. Likewise, we need to go wherever the Lord sends us and pray for people so they will all be healed. He may send you to the mall. He sent me to the grocery store.

As a believer, Jesus is with you all the time because He lives in you. By staying plugged into Him, you have the mind of Christ and can know exactly what to do and say even at the grocery store. Have you ever considered praying for a person in public? Maybe you think healing the sick should be a private matter. When you approach someone who needs prayer, do not hesitate. Don't pass by as you silently say a prayer. God does not get the glory or the credit when a miracle happens in secret. Giving Him the glory following a miracle is important and should not be neglected.

Many people take on the responsibility for the sick person's healing. They tell themselves, "What if I pray and the person doesn't get healed?" I have found that this is the number one excuse for believers' not praying for others. Jesus instructed us to *"lay hands on the sick, and they will recover"* (Mark 16:18). He did not tell His followers that healing was their responsibility. He instructed them to pray and lay hands on the sick. It is God's responsibility to heal the person or change the situation.

Would Jesus walk up to a person in the neighborhood mall who needed healing and, at the last moment, hesitate and turn away thinking, "What if he doesn't get healed?" That would never happen. Jesus was always led by the Holy Spirit. When He ministered in the marketplaces of His day, He never doubted the Father would heal through Him. He knew His authority and walked in it all the way to the cross and into our lives and hearts.

Do you feel comfortable praying for someone at church, yet avoid approaching a sick or hurting person in a grocery store? Do you dream you will serve God overseas someday, but you have never done anything for Him at the mall or in your neighborhood? Start where Jesus has you *today*. Ask Him to open your spiritual eyes and ears to the immediate needs around you. Remember, *"...Behold, **now** is the accepted time; behold, **now** is the day of salvation"* (2 Cor. 6:2).

Therefore, Go

Today God is sending you to the marketplace. God is sending you to your job. He is sending you to your neighborhood. He is raising you up to lead your whole family to Jesus. Do not allow anything to hold you back. Let me give you an example.

A student in an upstate New York Bible college had a serious speech impediment. Although he felt called to the ministry, professors and leaders at the Bible college privately expressed concerns that the student's disability could interfere with his effectiveness on the mission field.

Graduation day rolled around, and the student stood at the podium before his class, professors, visitors, and school leaders. He opened his Bible and read from Luke 4:18, *"The Spirit of the Lord is upon Me, because He has anointed Me...."* The Holy Spirit touched the young man, and he began weeping loudly, unable to go on. Then the Holy Spirit fell with power on the audience and they all began weeping, praising God, and praying. When this young man heard God's call, he could have looked at his infirmity and said, "I can't." Instead, he looked to Jesus, who said, "You can!"

When someone cries out, "God, if You're real, send somebody to tell me," I want you to be the one who readily responds, "Here am I. Send me."

The Right Place at the Right Time

I put the "Do not disturb" sign on my hotel door one afternoon when I suddenly had the feeling that I had to replace my dirty towels as soon as possible. I picked up the dirty linens and opened the door leading to the hallway. I immediately ran into the housekeeper. She was in need. I prayed for her and she was healed. If I had waited ten minutes to pray, seek a special word from God, or comb my hair to look "presentable," she would not have been there to receive her healing. I would have missed God.

To move in His anointing and authority requires obedience in every area of your life. Your every step needs to be ordained by Him. What if God wants to send you to the mall today, or anywhere else? He can order your steps. You have to listen and follow His leading. As you start each day with Him and stay in touch with the Holy Spirit, He will direct your steps. As you become more sensitive to Him, you will enter into the opportunities He has for you as well as the precautions to avoid the wrong path.

Learn to Prophesy

Ephesians 1:17-19 is a foundational Scripture for Joan Hunter Ministries. Read it in the light of First Corinthians 14:1-9, which says we are to desire to prophesy. One of the best ways to learn to prophesy is to speak His Word to yourself. When I get up in the morning, I point to myself in the bathroom mirror and prophesy according to the Word of God, "Today everything you put your hand to do will prosper" (see Ps. 1:3).

What does prophecy do for you? According to First Corinthians 14:3, "...*he who prophesies speaks edification and exhortation and comfort to men.*" Verse 31 continues, "...*you can all prophesy one by one, that all may learn and all may be encouraged.*"

The Scripture clearly indicates *"all"* can prophesy. That means you, me, and everyone else who reads His Word and believes. What does prophecy do? His Word tells us prophecy will encourage, edify, exhort, build up, stimulate, and give hope and comfort. Everyone needs that kind of encouragement!

When I speak words of prophecy over myself, I am also developing the prophetic gift within me. Reading the Word of God aloud prophetically, especially His promises, takes that Word from the future and brings it to the here and now. Point to yourself and prophesy:

> *So God can point to us in all future ages as examples of the incredible wealth of His grace and kindness toward us, as shown in all He has done for us who are united with Christ Jesus* (Ephesians 2:7 NLT).

I am always amazed at how God fulfills His Word. All I am doing is quoting the Word of God over myself. It is a form of declaring, decreeing, and activating His Word prophetically. Prophesying works because it is based on the unshakable authority of His Word spoken with faith.

As the Word is fulfilled, God will use you as an example of His incredible wealth, favor, and kindness in all He has done for you through Christ Jesus. As you believe, think, and hear that Word spoken over you day after day, you will envision yourself following His directions and acting on it. You will know that today, beyond the shadow of a doubt, *"...my God shall supply all your need according to His riches in glory by Christ Jesus"* (Phil. 4:19).

An Equipping Prophetic Prayer

Read aloud Ephesians 1:17-19 over yourself. Speak and hear the Word of God. Point to the person in the mirror, and, as you prophesy over yourself, make it personal:

Today, God, the glorious Father of my Lord, Jesus Christ, is giving me a greater spirit of wisdom and revelation in the knowledge of Him, and in every area of my life—my finances, ministry, family, business, marriage, and relationships.

Today, God will give me greater spiritual wisdom and understanding of the wonderful future and the riches of the inheritance that He has for me. He will make me understand and lay hold of the incredible greatness of His power.

Father, open my spiritual eyes and ears so I can hear You more clearly and see people around me who are sick. Open my ears to hear their needs and groans, so I can lay hands on them and see them healed through Your mighty power, in Jesus' name. Amen.

Claim Your Inheritance

You have probably heard about receiving your inheritance when you die and go to Heaven. Actually, you don't get your inheritance when *you* die. Somebody else has to die before you get your inheritance. Ephesians 1:10-12 says that Jesus Christ died and has given you *His* inheritance. Everything He had on this earth and all He has in Heaven, is given to you to use— everything, even His name. Who is the executor of His will? Who is holding it back? Don't allow the enemy to claim what is legally and Scripturally yours. How do you lay hold of your inheritance? Claim it! Believe it! Use it!

I want you to walk in *all*—all Jesus died to give to you. *All* is inclusive of everything and excludes nothing. Jesus said He has given you *all* His authority. Are you going to turn around and say, "Well, Lord, maybe it would be nice if You did what Your Word says," or "God, I believe in Jesus, but I'm not so sure that I can use His name," or "If it is Your will, please heal this person"? No. Follow Jesus' example. He lives within you. He will work exactly the same way today as described in the Gospel—with *all* God's authority.

You understand authority. When your pastor says, "Sit down," you sit down. You recognize his authority. Because he is in authority, he doesn't need to jump up and down and yell at the top of his voice, "Sit down!" Likewise, you do not need to prove your authority or work up an emotional attitude. You just need to know your authority in Christ and His authority in you, speak to different diseases, and people will be healed, in Jesus' name.

You have received His inheritance. You are experiencing the exceeding greatness of His power toward you because you believe, all according to the working of His mighty power. Glory to God! God wants to use you right where you are. With your cooperation and obedience, He will take you beyond anything you could ever hope, dream, or imagine.

Jesus gave you all—all His authority, all His faith, all of His wisdom and knowledge. You need to walk in His promises.

HAVE YOU CONSIDERED:

1. Does Jesus live within your heart?_____
   _____
   _____

2. Do you want to follow His instructions? Without question or doubt? _____
   _____
   _____

3. Are you willing to do whatever He asks of you?
   _____
   _____
   _____

4. Do you trust Him to back up His promises?_____
   _____
   _____

5. Have you ever been healed by God?_____
   _____
   _____
   _____

6. Do you want to be more effective when you pray for the sick?_____
   _____
   _____
   _____

PART II

THE ROOT
CAUSES OF
DISEASES

When a paralyzed man was laid at His feet, Jesus' first con-
cern was not for the man's healing. First He said, "Man, your
sins are forgiven you" (Luke 5:20).

CHAPTER THREE

CLEANSING THE HEART

...Even now the ax is laid to the root of the trees...
(Luke 3:9).

The Parable of the Patio

When we originally moved into our home, we had a screened patio area in the back. Unfortunately, we could not fully enjoy it without special preparation. The screens did not keep out the dirt, rain, heat, humidity, or cold. I would love to sit out there in the winter, but I found it was too cold. My grandson liked to play out there in the summer, but it was too hot. The patio was big enough to handle 30 people, but the outdoor table had to be thoroughly scrubbed before our guests could enjoy a meal. We had a lovely room we couldn't use. We could not enjoy our beautiful backyard anytime we felt like.

We made a quality decision to change the environment of our patio. We invited workers into our home to tear down the screens, power wash the floor, and install airtight windows. After renovation, we now have a four-season room with air-conditioning and heat. The windows keep out the dirt, dust, humidity, rain, and snow. Now we can easily walk into the area anytime we choose and enjoy a clean, beautiful environment to entertain, talk, read, pray, or study.

The old patio can represent your life. The screens are tiny doors into your life that allow dirt and debris to enter. It is time to remove those screens, clean out the junk, and put up barriers to secure the doors and walls. Inviting God to supernaturally houseclean your heart is what my healing school is all about.

Jesus said that the heart is the source of uncleanness:

...What comes out of a man is what makes him "unclean." For from within, out of men's hearts, come evil thoughts, sexual immorality, theft, murder, adultery, greed, malice, deceit, lewdness, envy, slander, arrogance and folly. All these evils come from inside and make a man "unclean" (Mark 7:20-23 NIV).

When you come for ministry, you are inviting a change or a renovation in your life. When we minister healing to you, we are the workers who remove the screens, clean out the dirt, and secure the windows of your heart, mind, and body. Installing the protection of solid walls and healthy air keeps out the sin, trauma, word curses, generational curses, or other strongholds. We "power spray" your heart with the wind of the Holy Spirit, of whom Jesus said, *"...when He has come, He will convict the world of sin, and of righteousness, and of judgment"* (John 16:8). We wash you down with *"...the washing of water by the word"* (Eph. 5:26) so that you become *"...a glorious church, not having spot or wrinkle or any such thing, but that* [you] *should be holy and without blemish"* (Eph. 5:27).

Once the Word of God is spoken over you, it continues to release His precious promises into your life:

My son, do not forget my law, but let your heart keep my commands; for length of days and long life and peace they will add to you (Proverbs 3:1-2).

Sin Can Be an Open Door for Sickness

Before praying for or receiving healing, look for areas where sickness may have entered your life. Sin—disobedience, rebellion, bitterness, anger, unforgiveness, sexual sin, addiction, alcoholism, etc.—opens the door for the enemy to enter your life and ravage your body or mind with disease. Once a sin is identified, confessed, brought to the cross, and repented of, the sickness often leaves without prayer for healing. When the root cause is destroyed, the tree can't survive.

Jesus demonstrated this principle in Luke 5:17-26. While He was teaching, "*...the power of the Lord was present to heal them*" (Luke 5:17). When friends set a paralyzed man at Jesus' feet, He did not immediately pray for the man's healing. First He said, "*Man, your sins are forgiven you*" (Luke 5:20b). Then He addressed the man's physical infirmity. He said, "*Arise, take up your bed, and go to your house*" (Luke 5:24b).

Keep your heart pure before God, and you will be healed and retain your healing. Proverbs 4:23 states, "*Keep your heart with all diligence, for out of it spring the issues of life.*"

Bringing every sin to Him closes those doors through which the enemy could previously attack you. That sin no longer has power over you. This initial step is not a matter of condemnation, but of self-examination.

The Importance of Repentance

God has commanded you to "*choose life,*" not death (Deut. 30:19). A very important key to choosing life is your repentance from sin. "*...God has also granted to the Gentiles repentance to* life" (Acts 11:18). God does not want you, His precious child, trapped in the clutches of sin. He wants you healed and set free to enjoy the wonderful life He has created for you. Many are trapped by the subtle tentacles of sin. Despite a desire to be free from sin and disease, some don't want to be confronted or deal with their sin. Sin must be evicted from your life. Recognize it, repent of it, and kick it out.

Once you learn these principles, you will also reveal His truth to others who want to be free. You may be the person God wants to use to reach your neighbor down the street or your co-worker. Expect God to use you. Your words may be the only ones someone will listen to. Who will explain the freedom that comes with repentance of sins if you don't? Who will explain how to get free and healed if you don't? The apostle Paul asks the same question:

> How then shall they call on Him in whom they have not believed? And how shall they believe in Him of whom they have not heard? And how shall they hear without a preacher? And how shall they preach unless they are sent? As it is written: "How beautiful are the feet of those who preach the gospel of peace, who bring glad tidings of good things!" (Romans 10:14-15)

Prayers for purity are very important. David asked God to cleanse him not only from known sins, but also from hidden faults:

> Who can understand his errors? Cleanse me from secret faults. Keep back Your servant also from presumptuous sins; let them not have dominion over me. Then I shall be blameless, and I shall be innocent of great transgression (Psalm 19:12-13).

David's attitude pleased God. He called David "a man after My own heart" (Acts 13:22).

Jesus is coming back for a Church without spot or wrinkle. It is time to cleanse the house of God. Since He lives within you, you are His house. Your responsibility is to keep yourself clean and pure. Even if you have a good relationship with God, pray:

Father, I have sinned. I don't want to sin anymore and I repent. Take this sin of _____ from me and put it on the cross, never to be held against me. Father, I ask Jesus to come into my life, not just as my Savior, but also as my Lord. Through Your Holy Spirit, guide me into all that You have for me, in Jesus' name.

Rebellion and Addictions

A friend was once a prostitute, took drugs, and used alcohol. Some say, "Once an alcoholic, always an alcoholic," or "Once a drug addict, always a drug addict." No. Once she repented, broke the covenants with her past sexual partners, and was delivered from the spirit of rebellion, she was free. God purified her. She is a new creation.

Addictions stem from rebellion. They take the place of God in a person's life and violate the physical body, which is:

...the temple of the Holy Spirit who is in you, whom you have from God, and you are not your own? For you were bought at a price; therefore glorify God in your body and in your spirit, which are God's (1 Corinthians 6:19-20).

Whether the addiction is alcohol, drugs, food, tobacco, sex, video games, or shopping, compulsive addictions distract our focus and energy away from God, our spouses, our children, and our responsibilities. The enemy uses subtle ways to destroy us and keep us from doing God's will. Slowly, but surely, these addictions have devastating effects on mental and physical health, well-being, and relationships.

Addictions are innately a form of selfishness. People in bondage to addictions live for the fleeting temporary pleasure they experience. Destructive addictions such as drugs and alcohol sicken or kill you. Promiscuous sex not only can transmit deadly diseases, but it also destroys the foundation of marriage and family life. A more modern form of compulsion is Internet addiction. In South Korea, a growing number of adults and up to 30 percent of children under 18 are at risk; some have even died of exhaustion because they could not tear themselves away from the Web.[1] Who do you think is behind such addictions? Jesus said:

> *The thief* [devil] *does not come except to steal, and to kill, and to destroy. I* [Jesus] *have come that they may have life, and that they may have it more abundantly* (John 10:10).

Sometimes people turn to drugs or alcohol to numb the pain of a previous traumatic event in their lives, so prayer for those individuals should address trauma, fear, and pain. Once the causative issue is taken care of, the substance abuse is handled also.

Since the root of addiction is rebellion against God, repentance is the first step to being set free. If you have broken an addiction or other bad habit, yet you struggle with a desire to return to it again, the root of rebellion has not been destroyed.

Prayer Against Rebellion

> *Father, I have rebelled against You. I repent of this sin. Take it from me and put it on the cross of Jesus, never to be held against me, in Jesus' name. I renounce anything I said in rebellion against You, my parents, or others in authority over me. I repent of all those words. I break the power of the spirit of rebellion over me and command it to leave, in*

Jesus' name, never to return. Thank You, Jesus. Help me to obey You in all things and to always be led by Your Holy Spirit, in Jesus' name.

Prayer Against Addiction

Father, I confess my addiction to _____ and I ask Your forgiveness for this sin. I repent of _____. Cut my addiction to _____ from me now, in Jesus' name. I break its power over me and I put it on Your altar, never to return, in Jesus' name. I curse the spirit of trauma and fear, and I command all pain to leave, in Jesus' name. Father, I receive healing to (name any part of your body or mind that has been affected by the addiction) and I receive Your peace, in Jesus' name. Thank You, Jesus.

Prayer for Addiction to Prescriptions

Many people take medications prescribed by their physician. Occasionally, the body becomes dependent on a certain drug such as a pain medication. Pain from arthritic changes or deformities, back injuries, nerve injuries, or chronic headaches can seriously jeopardize a person's well-being as well as activity levels. Pain medications may have kept them functioning and comfortable for years. Without realizing it, a person unintentionally becomes addicted to that substance. You will pray for his or her total healing and freedom from the drugs; however, never tell someone to stop any prescribed medication. Caution the person to continue all medications until a physician gives permission to discontinue them. The doctor will decide when to change or stop a prescription drug. Removing the drugs too fast can cause serious problems.

Keep in mind, a documented healing becomes a strong witness to the doctor as well as to others. Doctors are often amazed that a miraculous healing has occurred after prayer.

Father, thank You that You have healed me (or the person you are praying for). I curse any addictions to prescription medicine and I command all side effects to go, in Jesus' name. Thank You, Jesus.

Anger and Bitterness

Repentance is also the first step to freedom and healing if you are dealing with anger or bitterness. When a spouse, employer, or other person does not meet your expectations, disappointment and anger rear their ugly heads. You withdraw and take back a bit of your heart. With each hurt, another brick goes up and soon a wall built with anger, resentment, unforgiveness, and bitterness has destroyed a relationship. Sometimes disappointments come from unmet expectations—good things that don't happen. More common are the instances of unfavorable circumstances—bad things that do happen.

Anger also erodes your relationship with God. People lose their jobs and blame God. A spouse stops going to church and the mate blames God. Someone in church betrays you and you blame God. You wonder, "Why did this happen? Did God do this to punish me?" You get angry and bitter and withdraw from God.

Restore Your Relationship With God

The circumstances or unmet expectations are caused by man, our flesh, or a spiritual attack. No matter what happens, God is always there for you. You are the one who moved. He didn't.

Be strong and of good courage, do not fear nor be afraid of them; for the Lord your God, He is the One who goes with you. He will not leave you nor forsake you (Deuteronomy 31:6).

Yet with each disappointment, you pull further away from God. You walk away—because of sin such as anger, disappointment, bitterness, or unbelief in God's love and in His Word (see Rom. 8:35). You wonder what happened to your relationship with Him. The enemy is very cunning as he creeps in with his lies to separate you from the source of all life and happiness.

There is good news. God wants to woo you back into a wonderful intimate relationship with Him. Pray and rededicate your life to Him right now:

> *Father, I have sinned. I repent. Take this sin from me now, and put it on the cross of Jesus Christ, never to be held against me again. Jesus, come into my life, not only as Savior, but also as Lord. Father, through Your Holy Spirit, guide me into all that You have for me. I have taken back part of my heart because of circumstances. I choose this day to give You my whole heart. I don't want to hold anything back. Amen.*

Restore Relationships With People

Human relationships are imperfect. For example, people tend to enter into marriage with unrealistic expectations. After a short time, the trash starts piling up. You tell your husband, "Take the trash out." He says, "No, I don't take out the trash." Your boss promises you a raise, but it never materializes. Your pastor doesn't meet your expectations. The leaders of the church don't recognize your contribution to the church or thank you for your volunteer work. Anger, bitterness, and resentment arise from these unmet expectations.

You have to lay down your unmet expectations. Instead of remaining angry, bitter, and resentful, react to unfavorable circumstances by dealing with these sins. Ephesians 4:26 says, *"In your anger do not sin: Do not let the sun go down while you are still angry"* (NIV). Jesus got angry. There are times when it is acceptable to get angry, but don't ever allow it to reach the point of sin. Verbal or physical abuse is never acceptable. Don't let your negative feelings fester—deal with the issue before the day ends. Practice forgiveness. Unforgiveness builds walls. Forgive the people who disappointed you, just as God forgives when you disappoint Him.

Prayer for Anger and Bitterness

Father, I lay down my unmet expectations of my spouse. In Jesus' name, I lay those unrealistic expectations on Your altar. Father, I lay down my unmet expectations of my children on Your altar, and I lay down my unmet expectations of my pastor. I lay down my unmet expectations of _____ (fill in the names of people who have disappointed you). And I lay down my unrealistic expectations of myself on Your altar. I release those who disappointed me. In Jesus' name.

ENDNOTE

1. Martin Fackler, "In Korea, a Boot Camp Cure for Web Obsesion," *New York Times*, November 18, 2007; http://www.nytimes.com/2007/11/18technology/18rehab.html; accessed September 16, 2010.

CHAPTER FOUR

BREAKING
PERSONAL STRONGHOLDS

Prayers for healing are often only one part of a person's restoration. Root causes of physical infirmities, mental illnesses, and emotional problems must be addressed as well. Many diseases can be traced to an event of severe trauma or high stress. For that reason, ministering healing often begins by dealing with *trauma.*

Trauma and stress can affect all areas of your body and mind. Your body's cells have cellular memory[1] that recalls and absorbs traumas until God sovereignly intervenes. In response to prayer, the trauma is cursed and its power broken.

Jesus also heals traumatic emotional memories and responses. Emotional issues, such as recurrent or irrational fear, is often traced to a situation from birth or childhood that is provoking the abnormal response.

PHYSICAL TRAUMA : Stress-Related Disease

There are two approaches to praying for trauma or stress-induced sickness. I can pray for necks, backs, and other illnesses brought on by stress such as irritable bowel syndrome, acid reflux, ulcers, Crohn's disease, heart attacks, strokes, high blood pressure, diabetes, ulcers, and sleep apnea, just to name a few. Or I can tell you how to get rid of stress, and you won't have to pray over those illnesses again.

Stress is part of life. The source can come from family, finances, job, church, accidents, injuries, hospitalization, friends, strangers…and more. Research shows that 75 percent of visits to doctors' offices are stress-related.[2] Getting rid of stress often becomes more important than praying for somebody's neck or back, even though you need to minister to both problems. To be healed and stay healed, identifying the root cause of a disease is essential.

A man had been seriously injured in a traumatic car accident several years before. He needed a new knee. Many people, including the man himself, had prayed for his knee to be healed. When he came to me for ministry, I chose not to pray for his knee. Hearing his story, I identified trauma as the root and knew that had to be taken care of before his knee could be restored. When I prayed, "In the name of Jesus, I curse that trauma and I command it to be gone," his knee was totally and instantly healed. Trauma is like a magnet to sickness—eliminate the trauma and the sickness will go away.

EMOTIONAL TRAUMA :
Rejection, Betrayal, Unforgiveness, and Fear

Some people want to die because they can no longer endure the pain in their heart. They believe a serious illness is God's way of taking them off this earth so they don't have to live with that crippling pain anymore.

When a person cleanses him or herself of worry, unforgiveness, bitterness, anger, and the trauma that brought on the stress, that person's heart becomes clean and whole. With nothing to feed on, disease will leave. It is starved to death. Now, you are going to learn how to starve some diseases to death.

Reject Rejection

During a meeting in Oklahoma, two women were comparing their mid-sections to see whose was bigger. One was about eight months pregnant, the other was not pregnant. Their abdomens were nearly the same size. Through a word of knowledge about an abdominal problem, I called the woman who was not pregnant to the podium. She had 40 tumors in her stomach.

I prayed, "Father, I curse those tumors and command them to be gone, in Jesus' name." Immediately, she went from a size 18 down to a size 12. The Holy Spirit also revealed to me that she was dying on the inside.

When I place my hand near someone's heart, I can sense what is going on in his or her life. I put my hand over the woman's heart and prayed against spirits of trauma, rejection, abandonment, and abuse. She started crying. Her pastor was also crying as he repeated, "I love you, Suzie," and she was saying,

Place your hand over the heart when praying for emotional or physical healing.

"I love you, Pastor," back and forth. I asked her to repeat what her pastor said to her, and she answered, "I love you, Pastor."

"That's not what he said."

She started to say, "I love you…" but she couldn't speak.

I encouraged her, "Come on, you can say it."

She choked and almost gagged. Finally she repeated, "I love you, Suzie."

"Say it again," I said.

I had her repeat those words 15 to 20 times. I wanted to make sure she believed it. Why? She had a terrible self-image because all she saw was the abuse and shame of her past. In an instant, God changed her self-image. He not only set her free from her past, but He was also preparing her for His call on her life. She could not love others if she could not love herself.

If you are ashamed of what you look like and don't want to talk to anybody else, the last thing you want to do is minister to others. She used to wake up every morning, look at herself in the mirror, and say, "You are so ugly." Now she wakes up, looks in the mirror, and says, "I love you, Suzie. You are beautiful!"

A few days later, she joined us in Arkansas. Glowing and looking 20 years younger, she told us she would be back for service that night after getting something to eat. At the restaurant, she saw a man who was having great difficulty getting to his chair. Talking to the man, she learned he had a back problem that had caused excruciating pain for over ten years. He and his family came to the meeting that night, and the entire family was healed.

Her response is an example of what happens after you go through a healing school and receive your healing. When you see somebody in need, you will want to reach out to minister to that person. Some people's hands automatically extend toward the person in need, and others raise their hands in the Spirit. You will know when you walk in His anointing and direction. If this lady had not received healing of her wounded  self-image, she wouldn't have had the boldness to speak to the sick man. She had been too ashamed of herself to get out of her shell and pray for someone else. Her healing and restoration made her feel like a new creation. Her testimony gave many others the faith to believe for and receive their healing as well as the self-confidence to minister to others.

Overcoming Betrayal

If you have ever been betrayed, you are in good company. Jesus was betrayed. Paul was betrayed. Betrayal by a friend, spouse, or a member of your church is very painful. It is not the betrayal but how you react to it that counts, however. Your response to betrayal can affect your health because anger, bitterness, depression, and unforgiveness can eat away at your body and emotions, releasing stress hormones and weakening your immune system. What should you do if you have been betrayed?

Notice Paul's response to betrayal in Second Timothy 4:16-18:

At my first defense no one stood with me, but all forsook me. May it not be charged against them. But the Lord stood with me and strengthened me, so that the message might be preached fully through me, and that all the Gentiles might hear. Also I was delivered out of the mouth of the lion. And the Lord will deliver me from every evil work and preserve me for His heavenly kingdom. To Him be glory forever and ever. Amen!

Paul is a model of how to respond to betrayal. He did not let the effects of betrayal cling to him. What did he do? First, he prayed for those who had betrayed him (verse 16). This implies that he forgave them. Second, he relied on God instead of man and declared his faith in Him to deliver him *"from every evil work"* (verse 18). In effect, he put the negative situation behind him.

Jesus tells us, *"And whenever you stand praying, if you have anything against anyone, forgive him, that your Father in heaven may also forgive you your trespasses"* (Mark 11:25).

Unforgiveness keeps both you and the person who betrayed you in bondage. Forgiveness looses both of you. *"...Whatever you bind on earth will be bound in heaven, and whatever you loose on earth will be loosed in heaven"* (Matt. 16:19).

Prayer for Betrayal

Father, I forgive _____ for betraying me and I ask You to separate that sin from _____ and put it on the cross of Jesus, never to be held against _____ again, in Jesus' name. And Father, please forgive me of anger, bitterness, and unforgiveness toward _____. Put my sin on the cross, never to be held against me again. In the name of Jesus, I command the spirits of anger, bitterness, and rejection to leave me and I break their power over me. Thank You, Jesus, for Your promise, "'I will never leave you nor forsake you.' So [I] may boldly say: 'The Lord is my helper; I will not fear. What can man do to me?'" (Heb. 13:5-6).

Unforgiveness

Have you ever heard a child say, "I am sorry," without truly meaning what he or she said? Adults do the same thing when they go through the motions of forgiveness but don't forgive from the heart. Hurts and disappointments come from all directions. People can often hurt, reject by word or deed, criticize, or disappoint you. Unless you learn how to properly deal with your reactions, unforgiveness can grip your heart and become a stronghold.

Learning how to deal with unforgiveness often begins with your relationship with your parents. While some people grow up in dysfunctional families, even loving and well-meaning parents make mistakes in childrearing or fall short of their children's expectations. Some parents don't teach their children the value of forgiveness because they never learned or practiced it themselves.

Check your heart for bitterness. Is there anything you are still holding against your parents? Are you remembering something about your spouse, brothers, sisters, or other relatives? Perhaps friends, teachers, colleagues, bosses, or members of your church hurt you. Is there anyone you have not forgiven? As you think about each person, do you feel resentful, troubled, or peaceful? Offenses are part of life. The question is, how do you deal with that offense? You can choose to not take offense at the situation, and to instantly forgive and forget.

Jesus is our example. As He was crucified, He prayed, *"Father, forgive them, for they do not know what they do"* (Luke 23:34). Even as He endured suffering, Jesus interceded with the Father, mercifully pointing out the weakness of His tormentors. He also taught His disciples the importance of unequivocal and perfect forgiveness:

> *Then Peter came to Him and said, "Lord, how often shall my brother sin against me, and I forgive him? Up to seven times?" Jesus said to him, "I do not say to you, up to seven times, but up to seventy times seven. Therefore the kingdom of heaven is like a certain king who wanted to settle accounts with his servants. And when he had begun to settle accounts, one was brought to him who owed him ten thousand talents. But as he was not able to pay, his master commanded that he be sold, with his wife and children and all that he had, and that payment be made. The servant therefore fell down before him, saying, 'Master, have patience with me, and I will pay you all.' Then the master of that servant was moved with compassion, released him, and forgave him the debt"* (Matthew 18:21-27).

Jesus, "moved with compassion," forgave all your sins. Who are you to refuse to forgive others? Forgiving those who have sinned against you releases God's love and compassion to flow through you. The effect of this decision is peace in your heart and health in your body. If you choose not to forgive, the destructive effects of unforgiveness will boomerang on you. Unforgiveness is a poison that you drink, hoping that the other person is going to get sick. If you refuse to forgive, you are the one who will get sick. Unforgiveness leads to resentment, fear, and stress, which lowers the immune system and opens the door to arthritis and other diseases. Unforgiveness also keeps you in spiritual bondage. It clogs the conduit from you to God. You have to choose to end this never-ending cycle and clean this garbage out of your life. Jesus said:

> ...If you forgive men their trespasses, your heavenly Father will also forgive you. But if you do not forgive men their trespasses, neither will your Father forgive your trespasses (Matthew 6:14-15).

Go through your checklist and pray. Does the thought of any person on your list cause feelings of anger, bitterness, resentment, or discomfort? That could be a sign that you need to forgive him or her. Jesus told Peter to forgive people "not...seven times, but up to seventy times seven" (Matt. 18:22). Just as Jesus forgave those who killed Him, the Son of God, you are not to forgive based on who was right or wrong, but in obedience to God.

Prayer for Forgiveness

Father, I forgive _____ for hurting me. Separate this sin from _____ and put it on the cross, never to be held against_____ again. Father, bless _____. (Repeat this prayer for anyone else you need to forgive.)

I ask Your forgiveness for the anger, bitterness, and unforgiveness in my heart against_____. I receive Your forgiveness. Thank You, Father, in Jesus' name.

Face Your Fears

Asking for prayer, a woman told me her story. When she was three years old, her parents could not afford to care for her. They placed her in a children's home. When the home ran out of cribs, they put her in a regular bed. She would get out of her bed at night to talk to the other children in their cribs. The caregivers put her in a straightjacket, but she could still wiggle out of bed in the straightjacket. Finally, they put her in a straightjacket and strapped her to the bed. She could not get up in the middle of the night to go to the bathroom. It took a long time for her to learn not to relieve herself in bed.

I told her, "I want you to cross your arms over your chest."

She answered, "I can't, I can't, I can't, I can't."

I said, "If you give me less than three minutes, you'll be free."

Very reluctantly and breathing with great difficulty because of panic, she crossed her arms as if wrapped in a straightjacket. I put my arms around her, clasped my hands, and I squeezed her tighter than any straightjacket, saying, "I curse the spirit of trauma and fear. I command it to be gone, in Jesus' name."

As I released her, she crumpled to the floor. When she got up a few minutes later, I said, "Cross your arms again."

She reluctantly followed my instructions. Suddenly, a smile crossed her face as she said, "It's gone, it's gone, it's gone!"

That same day her marriage was healed. When she went home, she could totally love her husband for the first time. She endured all those years without a real hug because she panicked if her husband got too close. She was finally able to be close to her husband without anxiety attacks.

This woman is just one example of deliverance from the spirit of trauma and fear. When people come for ministry, there may be much more going on than you realize. People experience total restoration. They can get their lives back. Fear stole this woman's life from her when she was only three years old. She prayed for deliverance from fear for years. Once she was free, she wept for joy over the grace and mercy of God.

God wants you to get your life back and be totally free.

Prayer to Take Your Life Back

With the authority that Jesus Christ has given you, put your hand on your heart and pray:

Father, in the name of Jesus, I curse the spirits of trauma and fear, anxiety, hopelessness, depression, oppression, rejection, abandonment, loss, spirit of grief, and worthlessness. I command all that to go away. All feelings of worthlessness, that I will never amount to anything, I command them to go away, in Jesus' name. Go, fear of failure, never doing anything right, abuse, physical abuse, verbal abuse, loss of job, or loss of income, in the name of Jesus.

When you start this cleansing prayer, your heart may be full of pain and grief, but as you pray, it will become empty. In the name of Jesus, fill it back up.

Father, in the name of Jesus, I speak love, hope, rest, peace of mind, and no more loss. I speak this over myself with Jesus' authority and receive restoration and health to my body, health to my spirit, and health to my mind. Allow my heart, layer upon layer, to be filled with God's love. Fill my heart, Lord, with only You. Thank You, Jesus.

Healing Mental Illnesses

Not only can trauma trigger physical diseases, it can also cause mental illnesses like schizophrenia, bipolar disorder, and agoraphobia.

During one healing school, a man (I will call him Sam), came up for ministry. We prayed, laid hands on him, and anointed him. I felt led to pray, "Father, in the name of Jesus, I curse the spirit of trauma and fear." I also prayed for his freedom from other bondages.

Later that afternoon I found out that Sam had been labeled "the church schizophrenic," and I mentioned that schizophrenia is caused by trauma. He revealed his story. When he was three years of age, his mother poured gasoline over herself, struck a match, and died in a burst of fire in front of him. His father got legal custody of Sam. His mother's suicide was minor compared to what his father did to him. After we prayed for Sam, he was completely set free.

A few days later Sam came to the midweek service and gave his testimony. He lived in a home for people with special needs. Residents are supervised 24/7 but can be brought to church.

Sam explained he was finally allowed to have nail clippers in supervised surroundings, so he was allowed to cut other residents' toenails. A man came in and lay down on the table. Sam noticed one leg was shorter than the other.

Sam asked, "Do you have a back problem?"

"Yes, I have pain in my back," the man said.

"Can I pray for you?"

He laid hands on the man's anklebones and said, "Father, I command this leg to grow and all the pain to go, in Jesus' name." The legs evened out.

Sam was so excited. He was trying to decide who he could share this experience with when a lady walked by. Her ankle was swollen, bright purple, and very painful.

"May I pray for your ankle?" Sam asked.

"Sure," she replied. Sam prayed. The swelling left and the color returned to normal instantly.

Sam did not stop there. He continued to lay hands on the sick and they were healed. All kinds of miracles happened. Imagine, the residents getting set free of trauma—and it all started when Sam was set free from the trauma he experienced as a small child.

Discarded by society and the opinions of man, Sam was not forgotten by God. As a glowing example of God's healing power, Sam proudly works for Him. People in his church are now saying, "If Sam can do it, we can do it, too!"

Prayer for Trauma

Put your hand on your heart (or over the heart of the person you are praying for) and pray:

In the name of Jesus, I curse the spirit of trauma and command it to go. I curse schizophrenia, bipolar syndrome, manic depression, agoraphobia, and anxiety (fill in what pertains to you or to the person), and I command it to go, in Jesus' name. I command the pH balance in _____ body to return to normal, for the electrical and magnetic frequencies to be in perfect harmony and balance, and for all chemicals to return to normal, in Jesus' name. I speak a strong, completely restored immune system and curse every prion in _____ body, in Jesus' name. Thank You, Jesus.

Grief and Loss

When my mom, Frances Hunter, was sick, she told me before she died, "Don't cancel a ministry date, and don't rush home to my body, because I'm not there. When you can, spend time with me while I'm alive, but don't cancel anything because I am dead."

She died on a Tuesday when I was away ministering. I flew home that Friday, went by the funeral home, signed papers, and told her body good-bye. That was one of the hardest things I have ever done. I then turned around, got on a plane, and went to Illinois to do a healing school. A few days later, I felt the heaviness of the trauma and grief overcoming me. I lost my voice, which is often the first thing to go after a trauma. I could pray for the sick, but I could not appear on television without a voice. I was scheduled to be on television the next morning. I had to have my voice back.

I was driving upstate. When I arrived in my hotel room, I got in the shower so I could cry out to God where no one but God could hear me. I could not even hear myself as I cried out, "In the name of Jesus, I rebuke this spirit of trauma. I rebuke the spirit of grief. You are not welcome here. You are trespassing and I command you to go in the name of Jesus!"

My voice was still gone. I said, "In the name of Jesus, I command my voice to return instantly!" As I said, "Hallelujah" at the top of my lungs, my voice was back.

The point is, I had a choice. I could have succumbed to the trauma and grief, but I chose not to do so. The situation could have incapacitated me and taken me off the road, possibly forever. But healing and wellness happen when you pray for trauma to go! I was healed! I was free AND God got ALL the glory!

Grief and loss can appear from all directions. Yes, the death of a loved one causes deep pain, which can totally overpower you and destroy your life. However, other events of life can also plant a seed of trauma into your heart and mind. Loss of anyone or anything which was very valuable and treasured can start the process. Separation from a good friend or loved one (such as those in the armed forces stationed around the world), job loss, disasters (floods, fires, hurricanes), death of a pet, theft of family mementos, home invasion, and car accidents are only a few examples of traumas that need to be dealt with through ministry.

Prayer for Grief and Loss

When there has been grief or loss, there is trauma. Put your hand on your heart and pray:

Father, in the name of Jesus, I curse the trauma caused by this grief and loss. I command it to go in Jesus' name, never to return. I curse the spirit of trauma and the spirit of grief and I break their power over me, in Jesus' name. I declare that I trust Your sovereign decision when to give and when to take life. I place my life and the life of everyone I care about in Your hands. I pray peace and joy into my heart, and I take for myself Your promise that "You have turned for me my mourning into dancing" (Ps. 30:11) and "sorrow and mourning shall flee away" (Isa. 51:11 KJV). Thank You, Jesus.

Guilt and False Responsibility

The wife of a man in his 40s divorced him and refused to allow visitation with his two small children. He moved in with his parents, who headed the healing ministry at their church. The man was diagnosed with cancer. The parents prayed and fasted, but their son died. They felt guilty and held themselves responsible for his death. They thought they had not had enough faith.

When someone has prayed for a spouse, child, or someone else who did not get healed; that person can feel he or she is at fault. Perhaps he did not do enough, perhaps she did not say the correct prayer, or perhaps he did not have enough faith. None of that is true.

These parents had been carrying full responsibility for their son's death for many years. That day, they were simply acknowledging what they had been doing for so long. I led them in this prayer: "I confess I took full responsibility for my son's cancer and death. I don't want to carry it anymore, and I lay that false responsibility and guilt on Your altar, Father, in Jesus' name."

God set them free! He then showed me why their son had died. Before his death, the man had said, "I would rather die than live with this terrible pain in my heart."

There are two lessons here. First, though God is pleased when we pray for someone's healing, He reminds us in His Word, *"I hold the keys of death..."* (Rev. 1:18 NIV). In the wilderness, God revealed a similar truth to Israel: *"I kill and I make alive; I wound and I heal; nor is there any who can deliver from My hand"* (Deut. 32:39b).

The second lesson is this: You need to understand trauma and grief. You can help set people free before they give in to hopelessness. The man believed the only way he could get over the pain in his heart was to check out of life. But God is compassionate and He restores. He wants to give people their lives back. You have to share the message because hopelessness and despair thrive all around you. The enemy uses whatever tactics he can to destroy.

Just as you have been released from the bondage of trauma, grief, stress, pain, and all the other negative slave masters that tormented you, you can use the same principles and prayers to reach others. When you identify those destructive symptoms in the lives of others, reach out, pray the same prayers over them, and see them recover.

ENDNOTES

1. For more on cellular memory, see Kate Ruth Linton, "Knowing by Heart: Cellular Memory in Heart Transplants," *Montgomery College Student Journal of Science and Mathematics* Vol. 2 (September 2003): http://www.montgomerycollege.edu/Departments /StudentJournal/volume2/kate.pdf.

2. "Factsheet: Mind Your Stress—On the Job," Mental Health America (2010): http://www.nmha.org/index.cfm?objectid= C7DF9974-1372-4D20-C89417A56B-38B3EF.

CHAPTER FIVE

BREAKING GENERATIONAL CURSES AND COVENANTS

As you mature in the Lord, you may have to unpack your spiritual baggage. Spiritual baggage includes curses passed down from previous generations. Generational curses can be sins such as anger or lying, or they can be addictions, traumas, or diseases. Do some research into your ancestors' lives.

Can you identify cancer in family members through the years? Is there evidence of mental illness? Is there a pattern of divorce, infidelity, or adultery? Did someone participate in witchcraft or the occult? Has poverty plagued your family tree over generations?

Repentance, prayer, and taking authority in Jesus' name will free you from generational curses as well as from harmful or invalid vows and covenants.

Generational Curses in the Bible

The Lord revealed to Moses that generational curses are real and can pass from generation to generation.

...The Lord, the Lord God, merciful and gracious, longsuf-
fering, and abounding in goodness and truth, keeping mercy
for thousands, forgiving iniquity and transgression and sin,
by no means clearing the guilty, visiting the iniquity of the

fathers upon the children and the children's children to the third and the fourth generation (Exodus 34:6-7).

In the events leading up to the crucifixion of Jesus, a generational curse began with a word curse:

When Pilate saw that he could not prevail at all, but rather that a tumult was rising, he took water and washed his hands before the multitude, saying, "I am innocent of the blood of this just Person. You see to it." And all the people answered and said, "His blood be on us and on our children" (Matthew 27:24-25).

Those people who answered Pilate had no idea what they were bringing upon their children and their children's children. Imagine being responsible for killing Jesus, the Son of God. What punishment they actually prophesied over their progeny! Their eyes were blinded by the enemy's hate of God.

Jeremiah and Ezekiel prophesied that a new covenant was coming when the vicious cycle of generational curses would be broken:

In those days they shall say no more: "The fathers have eaten sour grapes, and the children's teeth are set on edge." But every one shall die for his own iniquity; every man who eats the sour grapes, his teeth shall be set on edge. Behold, the days are coming, says the Lord, when I will make a new covenant with the house of Israel and with the house of Judah— ...But this is the covenant that I will make with the house of Israel after those days, says the Lord: I will put My law in their minds, and write it on their hearts; and I will be their God, and they shall be My people (Jeremiah 31:29-31,33).

"What do you mean when you use this proverb concerning the land of Israel, saying: 'The fathers have eaten sour grapes, and the children's teeth are set on edge'? As I live," says the Lord God, "you shall no longer use this proverb in Israel. ...

Yet you say, 'Why should the son not bear the guilt of the father?' Because the son has done what is lawful and right, and has kept all My statutes and observed them, he shall surely live. The soul who sins shall die. The son shall not bear the guilt of the father, nor the father bear the guilt of the son. The righteousness of the righteous shall be upon himself, and the wickedness of the wicked shall be upon himself" (Ezekiel 18:2-3;19-20).

Daniel, Ezra, and Nehemiah all prayed to break generational (and national) curses. After Daniel confessed his sins and those of his fathers and Israel's leaders, he prayed:

O Lord, according to all Your righteousness, I pray, let Your anger and Your fury be turned away from Your city Jerusalem, Your holy mountain; because for our sins, and for the iniquities of our fathers, Jerusalem and Your people are a reproach to all those around us. ...O Lord, hear! O Lord, forgive! O Lord, listen and act! Do not delay... (Daniel 9:16,19).

Ezra also acknowledged, *"Since the days of our fathers to this day we have been very guilty..."* (Ezra 9:7). When Nehemiah learned of the devastation of Jerusalem, he confessed *"the sins of the children of Israel which we have sinned against You. Both my father's house and I have sinned"* (Neh. 1:6b).

When Jesus died on the cross, the new covenant Jeremiah and Ezekiel had foreseen was set in place, and the power of generational curses was broken once and for all. We can pray in the authority of His atonement when we break generational curses and diseases.

You can be blinded by the enemy when you speak a negative word, a vow, or a false promise. Learn to protect yourself and those you love. Think before you speak. Break those curses from your life and off your loved ones.

Prayer for Generational Sins

Father, I repent for my sins and the sins of my fathers. Take this sin from us and put it on the cross, never to be held against us again. The generational curse of _____ and the destructive habit of _____ are now broken off of me, in Jesus' name. Thank You, Jesus.

Prayer for Generational Diseases

When you pray against physical and natural problems that have affected generations of your family, be specific. For example, pray: *The generational curse of cancer* _____ (name the disease or symptom) *is now broken off of me. Poverty* _____ (fill in your situation) *is broken off me. Thank You, Jesus.*

Transfusions and Transplants

Since generational curses are passed down through the bloodline, they can attach to a person by means of a blood transfusion, gamma globulin, human-derived insulin, or a body part transplant.

I once read a story about a heart transplant patient who received a heart from someone who loved to ride horses. The patient had never been on a horse before. Since she received the heart transplant, she loves riding horses. Positive attributes can be transferred as well as negative ones.

After one young girl received a heart, she started having repetitive nightmares about a specific license plate. She could not understand why she was having nightmares. Her family decided to check out the license plate number. It belonged to the uncle of the young girl who had died and had become the heart donor. The police followed the lead and checked out the uncle's car. They found bloodstains and the DNA of his niece.

He had abducted her, beaten her, and thrown her into the trunk. Apparently the last thing that she was aware of before being put in the trunk was the license plate number. Thinking she was dead, the uncle disposed of her body. She was rescued but did not survive. As a result of this investigation, the man was convicted of murder and imprisoned. This is just one example of how the power of trauma from one person can come into another through cellular memory.

Prayer for Donating Blood

I am a proponent not only of blood transfusions if you need one, but also of blood and plasma donation. I believe that you are donating blood that is full of the Holy Spirit and free of generational curses. As you give, pray, "Father, in the name of Jesus, thank You for anointing this blood to accomplish Your purpose. Thank You that it will go to the right recipient who needs to know You."

So shall My word be that goes forth from My mouth; it shall not return to Me void, but it shall accomplish what I please, and it shall prosper in the thing for which I sent it (Isaiah 55:11).

Prayer for Transfusions, Transplants, or Insulin

Several years ago, I had a root canal. From the age of 12 until a few years ago, I suffered from multiple tooth infections. An oral surgeon found a golf-ball sized cyst in my head that had destroyed part of my skull. To remedy it, the surgeon removed the cyst and sprinkled cadaver bone in the spot. New bone formed perfectly around the particles.

After the transplant, I prayed, "Father, right now, take any generational curses from me or sins or trauma attached to this bone, in Jesus' name."

What happened next was like seeing rain hitting asphalt and steam rising on a hot Texas day. I said, "Did you see that?" to the person who was there with me. We physically saw something leave me. I was very glad I prayed that prayer.

Take authority in the name of Jesus over anything that may have entered with a blood transfusion, transplant, gamma globulin, or human insulin.

> *Father, I repent for my sins and the sins of the person whose*
> *_____ I received. Take this sin and put it on the cross of*
> *Jesus Christ never to be held against us again, in Jesus' name.*
> *Any generational curses that came in through this_____*
> *is cut off from me now, in Jesus' name. Thank You, Jesus.*

Remember, when you pray for yourself or others, pray with the authority that Jesus has given to you. He told His disciples in Matthew 18:18: "...*Whatever you bind on earth will be bound in heaven, and whatever you loose on earth will be loosed in heaven."* In the book of John, Jesus said to them, "...*Receive the Holy Spirit. If you forgive the sins of any, they are forgiven them; if you retain the sins of any, they are retained"* (John 20:22-23).

Vows and Covenants

God considers marriage a holy covenant. The covenant is not formed during the wedding or at the church. The covenant is formed and finalized later in bed. The blood shed at the breaking of the woman's hymen is the sign of the covenant of marriage. If a spouse dies, the marriage covenant is broken by death. When a couple gets divorced, they must verbally renounce that covenant.

There has been a lot of teaching in the church about breaking soul ties after a divorce or other intimate relationship. In post-divorce counseling, I was advised to renounce the soul ties between me and my ex-husband. Although there is nothing wrong with this prayer, soul ties are not a scriptural concept. When you got married, you did not go into soul ties with your spouse—you went into covenant. I believe that soul ties are a symptom of that covenant.

When I prayed, "I break the soul ties, in Jesus' name," I felt a little better. However, I was still in covenant with a man who was doing many ungodly things, and I was trying to minister while still carrying that burden. When the reality hit and I knew the truth, I was not in covenant five minutes longer. I renounced that covenant at once. What a difference breaking that covenant made! I was free!

If you have been through a divorce, renounce the covenant you made with your previous spouse. The prayer will set both partners free from the covenant.

Prayer for the Divorced

Father, I went into a godly covenant with _____. Now that I am divorced, I renounce that covenant. Anything bad that came in through that covenant, take it from me now, in Jesus' name. Thank You, Jesus.

Prayer to Break Ungodly Covenants

The same principle applies to any person with whom you have had sexual intercourse other than your marriage partner. Paul explains the scriptural foundation for sexual purity in his epistle to the church at Corinth:

...Now the body is not for sexual immorality but for the Lord, and the Lord for the body. ...Do you not know that your bodies are members of Christ? Shall I then take the members of Christ and make them members of a harlot? Certainly not! Or do you not know that he who is joined to a harlot is one body with her? For "the two," He says, "shall become one flesh." But he

who is joined to the Lord is one spirit with Him. Flee sexual immorality. Every sin that a man does is outside the body, but he who commits sexual immorality sins against his own body. Or do you not know that your body is the temple of the Holy Spirit who is in you, whom you have from God, and you are not your own? For you were bought at a price; therefore glorify God in your body and in your spirit, which are God's (1 Corinthians 6:13,15-20).

Ungodly sexual covenants are formed not only with flesh and blood partners, but also with fantasy partners—by pornography, masturbation, or reading explicit romance novels. The Word of God is clear: If a man has done it in his heart, he has done it. Jesus is coming back for a pure Church without spot or wrinkle (see Eph. 5:27). He said He wants not only our bodies pure, but our thought life as well. *"...Whoever looks at a woman to lust for her has already committed adultery with her in his heart"* (Matt. 5:28). Paul also exhorts us to bring *"every thought into captivity to the obedience of Christ"* (2 Cor. 10:5b). Pray:

Father, I went into an ungodly covenant with _____. I repent for that sin. Take it from me now and put it on the cross, never to be held against me again. I renounce that covenant in Jesus' name. Anything bad that came in through that covenant, take it from me now, in Jesus' name. Thank You, Jesus.

If you have had a promiscuous lifestyle and you cannot remember specific names, as God reminds you, renounce each covenant in Jesus' name.

Some covenants are the result of molestation that resulted in intercourse. You need to break these unwanted covenants and forgive the person who abused you:

Father, I was forced into an ungodly covenant with _____. I forgive _____ for that sin. Take it from _____ now and put it on the cross, never to be held against _____

again. I renounce and break that covenant in Jesus' name. Anything bad that came in through that covenant, take it from me now, in Jesus' name. I command the trauma, fear, shame, and guilt of that experience to go, in Jesus' name. Thank You, Jesus.

Blood Covenants

Children may make blood covenants by pricking their fingers and exchanging blood, becoming "blood brothers." Doors to generational curses can be opened through something as simple as pricking your finger as a child. Break that covenant. Perhaps the other person is living for the devil and you do not understand why living for Jesus has been difficult for you. Your covenant partner's actions do affect you. If this has happened to you, pray:

Father, in Jesus' name, I renounce the covenant I made with _____. Please forgive us for this sin and take it from us and put it on the cross of Jesus, never to be held against us again. I break that covenant off of me in the name of Jesus. Anything bad that came in through that covenant, take it from me now, in Jesus' name. Thank You, Jesus.

Spiritual Transfers

Curses or spiritual oppression can be passed on spiritually as well as physically. Sometimes people who mean well lay hands on others and pray. If the Holy Spirit is not the source of their prayers, their words and possibly their demonic oppressions can be passed on to you. Exposure to the occult can have a similar effect, whether you have been a participant or were an innocent bystander.

If either of these situations has happened to you or to others you are praying for, pray:

Father, anything that came upon me by the laying on of hands that wasn't from You, take it from me now, in Jesus' name. I cut off any curses or spiritual bondages and receive only what comes from Your hand. Thank You, Jesus.

And Father, I renounce my involvement in (the occult practice of) _____. I repent. I renounce any words I spoke or that others spoke over me during those practices, in Jesus' name. Take from me now any influences or oppressions that came against me. I cast them away from me and nullify them, in Jesus name. Thank You, Jesus.

CHAPTER SIX

CURSES AND BLESSINGS

The Power of Your Words

God formed the world with His Word. We form our world with our words.

Deuteronomy 30:19 says, *"...I have set before you life and death, blessing and cursing; therefore **choose life**, that both you and your descendents may live."*

One way you *choose life* is by carefully choosing your words. There is power in words. God spoke and the world was created. He demonstrated the importance of spoken words when He overturned the scheme of Balak, the king of Moab, who hired the false prophet Balaam to curse Israel. God turned Balaam's curses into blessings.

Then the Lord put a word in Balaam's mouth, and said, "Return to Balak, and thus you shall speak." So he returned to him, and there he was, standing by his burnt offering, he and all the princes of Moab. And he took up his oracle and said: "Balak the king of Moab has brought me from Aram, from the mountains of the east. 'Come, curse Jacob for me, and come, denounce Israel!' How shall I curse whom God has not cursed? And how shall I denounce whom the Lord has not denounced? For from the top of the rocks I see him, and from

the hills I behold him; there! A people dwelling alone, not reckoning itself among the nations. Who can count the dust of Jacob, or number one-fourth of Israel? Let me die the death of the righteous, and let my end be like his!" Then Balak said to Balaam, "What have you done to me? I took you to curse my enemies, and look, you have blessed them bountifully!" (Numbers 23:5-11)

God wants to turn your curses into blessings as well. For this to happen, you must understand the importance of words. The Scriptures bear witness to the powerful effect that words have on people. Proverbs 18:21 states, *"Death and life are in the power of the tongue, and those who love it will eat its fruit."*

An example of this truth in a person's life took place at a service in Canada where the Lord gave me a word of knowledge. I said, "Someone recently lost a loved one, and your body is falling apart. You were married for a long time. Now you feel like you are dying. Who is that?"

A female pastor came forward. Her husband of 45 years had died a year and a half earlier. After his death, she experienced one illness after another. Her diseases were caused by trauma and grief.

At the prompting of the Holy Spirit, I asked, "Did you ever say to your spouse, 'I don't want to live without you?'"

That comment sounds romantic, but it is not. The woman had unknowingly made a vow of death over her life. I had her renounce her vow and I prayed against the spirit of trauma and grief. I did not pray for her physical problems because the pain had already left her body.

You may not want to live without your spouse, but you can. If you have made that vow, pray: *"I renounce that vow with death, in Jesus' name."*

Speak Words That Bless

Have you ever said words or had words spoken over you that did not edify, exhort, correct in love, or confirm?

God gave me a prophetic word for a man: "God says He's really proud of you, and you're a good man." He started crying uncontrollably.

"You've never heard that from your natural father, have you?" I asked.

His father had always told him he was a bad boy, a bad man, a bad father, and a bad husband. He felt powerless to overcome those words. He lived "down" to what he believed about himself.

Many word curses have been spoken over me. I had problems accomplishing anything because I was told most of my life that I was retarded and would never amount to anything. A teacher once told my mother that I was the dumbest student who had ever attended that particular elementary school. My mother accepted that opinion because of the authority of my teachers.

When Mom and Dad first met, Dad would call and I answered the phone with the words, "Hi, this is Dumb Dumb."

He told me, "Don't say that! I'm going to call you Smart Smart." And he did!

When I removed the labels of "stupid," "dumb," and "ignorant," all Heaven broke open for me. I am none of those things. I had believed the lies of the devil. I renounced those words and became what I believed.

Destructive words can also affect a person's health. If you have been diagnosed with ADD or labeled with negative names, God can take away the limits and the pain of your past. He did it for me. Not only was I healed and set free, but God also turned those curses around and blessed me instead. Are you ready to become what you believe God wants you to be?

Beware of Judging or Criticizing

Luke 6:38 says to give and you will receive. In context, this Scripture applies not only to finances—it also speaks about judging and forgiveness:

> *Judge not, and you shall not be judged. Condemn not, and you shall not be condemned. Forgive, and you will be forgiven. Give, and it will be given to you: good measure, pressed down, shaken together, and running over will be put into your bosom. For with the same measure that you use, it will be measured back to you* (Luke 6:37-38).

Judge or withhold forgiveness and you will be judged and remain unforgiven. Love and you will be loved—pressed down, shaken together, running over. When you judge, condemn, gossip, or refuse to forgive, what is in your heart comes out of your mouth. Those words cut off your blessings by coming back on you. *"As he loved cursing, so let it come to him; as he did not delight in blessing, so let it be far from him"* (Ps. 109:17). Whatever you sow, you will reap. This includes accepting and repeating a negative report from a doctor, accountant, etc.

Think before you speak, judge, or criticize. Plant love and reap His blessings!

Prayer to Break Word Curses

> *Father, I have said words that didn't edify, exhort, correct in love, or confirm. That is sin. Take this sin from me and put it on the cross, never to be held against me again. I renounce those words, in Jesus' name. Bless anybody I said these words about, in Jesus' name.*

I also forgive the people who spoke words over me that did not edify, exhort, correct in love, or confirm. Separate those sins from them and put them on the cross, never to be held against them again. Those words and their effects, including the words of doctors or their reports, are cut off from me now, in Jesus' name. Father, bless everyone who spoke negative words over me, in Jesus' name.

Now proclaim blessings over your life to counteract any curses. For example, you can say, "I am going to live and not die, and declare the works of the Lord" (see Ps. 118:17). "I am prospering." "I am smart." "I am going to succeed." "My ministry will grow." "I will lay hands on the sick and they will recover" (see Mark 16:18).

You may need to repeat this prayer over specific areas such as your finances, job, family, or health. Choose life in all areas of life and cut off all negative words in the name and the authority of Jesus. Those negative word curses will have no more power over you.

After you rebuke and cut off the illness or condition, speak the opposite of what has been afflicting them. Command peace, life, joy, health, prosperity, wholeness, and the love of God to fill them—that they will *"know the love of Christ which passes knowledge; that* [they] *may be filled with all the fullness of God"* (Eph. 3:19).

Testimonies

Sometimes the Holy Spirit will reveal to you a root cause that opened the door to the disease. In the case of this man's story, word curses were just one root source of the disease. A man suffering with cancer could not even walk down the church aisle. His joints were destroyed and unable to function normally. His cancer had started in his chest wall. Surgeons had removed part of his left lung and some ribs. Doctors had told him he had eight years to live—and his eight years were up. His chest was causing him serious pain, which increased his fear. I prayed:

Father, in the name of Jesus, I curse the spirit of trauma and fear. I command it to be gone. I curse this cancer and every prion—infectious pathogens that cause degenerative diseases of the brain and nervous system—in this body, and I speak complete restoration, in Jesus' name.

Father, in the name of Jesus, I speak a whole new left lung. I speak complete restoration, in Jesus' name, of this body, and the lung in particular, and I command all pain and any damage as a result of surgery or medicine to go. I speak health and wholeness and complete restoration, in Jesus' name.

Then I led the man in the following prayer, having him repeat it after me, one phrase at a time:

Father, I have said words that were not nice words. I repent for those words and for that sin. Take it from me now and put it on the cross, never to be held against me again. The doctors in particular spoke words to me that weren't very nice. They said I only had eight years to live, which is just a few seconds away. In the name of Jesus, I cut those words off. I am going to live several more years, in Jesus' name, and they are going to be healthy years. I am going to be a sign and a wonder to the doctors. Thank You, Jesus.

We broke the word curse over him in Jesus' name. His bones, which had been frozen and fused, were loosed. His pain was gone! At last report, his pastor says he is riding his bike. He has his life back because he broke the curse that doctors had spoken over him. He agreed with all the positive words we spoke.

How God Turned a Curse Into a Blessing

People may have told you, "Learn to live with your illness or it will kill you." Do not believe those destructive words! Do not accept that curse! It is up to you to *choose life.*

When my words are aligned with the Word of God, they have the power to turn curses into blessings. I had to learn to live this truth. You can also. Revelation 12:10-11 states:

...the accuser of our brethren, who accused them before our God day and night, has been cast down. And they overcame him by the blood of the Lamb and by the word of their testimony, and they did not love their lives to the death.

Notice that *"the word of* [our] *testimony"* plays a role in casting down satan, the accuser of the brethren. I had to lay hold of that truth when I was diagnosed with breast cancer just two days after my divorce was finalized.

When I was diagnosed with breast cancer, I immediately saw myself in the ground and planned what I was going to wear in the casket. My next thought was, "My girls need me." I slapped my face as hard as I could to knock some sense into my head. I started proclaiming the Word of God and chose to get the spirit of death out of the room. Over and over, I said, "I am going to live and not die and declare the works of the Lord! I choose life!" (See Psalm 118:17; Deuteronomy 30:19.)

When I got rid of resentment, unforgiveness, bitterness, worry, and stress, I starved the cancer. I did not have to have surgery or chemo. God even took away the scar from the biopsy.

Anyone diagnosed with cancer or any other disease should repeat, "I choose life. I shall live and not die and declare the works of the Lord. I choose life. I choose life. I shall live and not die and declare the works of the Lord."

When you pray the Word of God with faith over others, you can see and feel the heaviness and the spirit of death leave them. If you know anybody who has cancer or another disease, curse the sickness and speak a new body part, in Jesus' name. Ask the person to repeat what I said, "I choose life. I will live and not die. I will declare the works of the Lord."

Some of you may need to repeat this prayer in other areas as well. For instance, you may have spoken death over your finances, your job, a family member, or your health because you agreed or submitted to a word curse spoken by a teacher, a doctor, or someone else.

For instance, if you have ever said, "I will never have enough, I cannot find a better job, my kids will never succeed, I will never get healed," renounce those words and start speaking positive words of life over all areas of your life. Watch for and document what happens over the next months. Let me know what God does for you!

General Healing Prayer

Pray this prayer every morning and night for wholesomeness and total health. Praise and thank Him continuously for your healing.

In the name of Jesus, I command all 125 trillion cells along with all the T-cells in my body to align electrically, magnetically, and chemically to the perfect DNA and RNA that God created. I curse any prions and antigens in this body. I command all the bad cells to be discarded, in Jesus' name. Thank You, Jesus! Amen.

Now that I have learned this powerful truth through personal experience, I can teach you these principles of choosing life and renouncing words of death!

I walk in victory and wholeness. You can, too!

PART III

GOD'S WISDOM FOR VIBRANT HEALTH AND WEALTH

Beloved, I wish above all things that thou mayest prosper and be in health, even as thy soul prospereth (3 John 2 KJV).

CHAPTER SEVEN

NURTURE THE NATURAL MAN
DR. S. LUSSIER, NMD
(www.inspiremedicine.com)

God created us to live in harmony with others and the environment. He gave us free will to choose what to allow into our bodies, minds, and spirits. The first people who had to make those choices were Adam and Eve. When it came to deciding what to eat, God gave them all that they needed—fresh organic produce and clean spring water—right in their backyard. Yet they chose to eat the one thing God commanded them not to eat.

> *And the Lord God commanded the man, saying, "Of every tree of the garden you may freely eat; but of the tree of the knowledge of good and evil you shall not eat, for in the day that you eat of it you shall surely die"* (Genesis 2:16-17).

How many of us can relate to this? Every day we have numerous choices about what to eat. Our environment has changed dramatically since the time of Adam and Eve. Not all of us have organic gardens growing in our backyard. Although we do have access to healthy options, we often choose less healthy ones instead. Why? There are a few reasons why bad habits have become the norm.

The Trap of "Convenience" Foods

The first is convenience. How often are we rushing through our day and feel we need to grab and go? We assume there is not enough time to cook a healthy meal. If you think about it, by the time you decide where you are going, drive there, wait at a restaurant or a drive-thru, and finally get your food, the process may actually take longer than cooking a healthy meal. Cooking at home is becoming a lost art due to the rampant fast-food culture around us. Discover the joy and creativity of cooking using fresh ingredients, and you will reap the reward of good health. You will also have the peace of mind that comes with knowing exactly what is in your food.

Discern True Value

A second reason for choosing unhealthy food options is cost. Many people look at the price tag of a healthy option and decide, "A $1 cheeseburger is a better value." But for those interested in true value, dollar for dollar, junk food is more expensive. Buying whole foods and preparing them at home costs less than quick convenience foods. The savings really add up when you compare the costs and rewards of preventing obesity, diabetes, high blood pressure, heart disease, and even cancer. The next time you look at the price tag of convenient junk food, add in the real cost of eating these unhealthy foods, and your decision will be much easier. You will understand the real value of making healthier choices.

Why spend money on what is not bread, and your labor on what does not satisfy? Listen, listen to Me, and eat what is good, and your soul will delight in the richest of fare (Isaiah 55:2 NIV).

Educate Yourself

The last reason that people choose unhealthy options is the lack of knowledge. The Scripture says, *"My people are destroyed for lack of knowledge..."* (Hos. 4:6). Isn't this true of the nutritional choices today? People make poor decisions because they honestly don't know better. Some learned bad habits along the way and don't know how to begin over or where to start.

Many companies are profiting from the public's ignorance by using deceptive marketing. Ads and product containers highlight product features such as "low fat," "no sugar added," "whole grain," and "no trans fats." While these attributes are wholesome and healthy features, they often disguise harmful contents hidden in the ingredient list. Even when someone thinks he is making good choices, he is often being compromised in some other manner. It doesn't have to be that way.

The Power of Choice

You have been given amazing power over your health by being able to choose your food and drink. The old saying, "You are what you eat," is really true. You choose the raw materials that your body has to work with. Every cell of your brain, heart, skin, joints, and every other organ in your body is produced by the food and drinks you choose to put in your mouth. Are you giving your body optimal building blocks or are you building a weak foundation that is prone to weakness and disease?

Eating unhealthy foods is like building a house on sand. It may stand for many years without problems, but when the storms come, that house will crumble.

Therefore whoever hears these sayings of Mine, and does them, I will liken him to a wise man who built his house on the rock: and the rain descended, the floods came, and the winds blew and beat on that house; and it did not fall, for it was founded on the rock. But everyone who hears these sayings of Mine, and does not do them, will be like a foolish man who built his

house on the sand: and the rain descended, the floods came, and the winds blew and beat on that house; and it fell. And great was its fall (Matthew 7:24-27).

The same is true for our bodies. If we spend many years eating poorly and not exercising, why are we surprised when disease strikes? We feel victimized, but instead we should be empowered to start rebuilding our foundation.

Build a Foundation for Wellness

Building a strong nutritional foundation is not difficult. It's all about making small changes and, much like building a house, it doesn't happen in one day. Many people make the mistake of an all-or-nothing attitude, and that is not sustainable. The only long-lasting action is making changes that you can live with. *"Do not despise these small beginnings"* (Zech. 4:10a NLT).

There are many schools of thought on what we can do to live better. We are constantly bombarded with the latest discovery of what is most beneficial for our health. I am always amazed at how many articles in respected medical journals find that a certain vitamin is beneficial. Reading them regularly, a common theme emerges: Eating a diet rich in fruits, vegetables, and lean protein, limiting processed foods, and participating in regular exercise results in healthier people.

Fruits and Vegetables

Fruits and vegetables are beneficial due to their antioxidants, protective molecules that prevent cell damage or aging. Everyone is regularly exposed to free radicals from the environment or from those produced by his or her own body. Free radicals are chemically unstable molecules due to an unpaired electron. They search throughout the body for molecules to bond with in order to become more stable. If they remain in the body, they can contribute to cell damage and aging,[1] or they may also form toxins that can lead to diseases like cancer.[2]

Antioxidants are an important defense against free radicals. They bind to these unstable free radicals and make them stable so they are no longer harmful to the body. Our main antioxidant defense is found in the food God put on the earth before we were created.

The most abundant source of antioxidants is the food group comprised of fruits and vegetables. Vitamins A, C, E, plus selenium, glutathione, and bioflavonoids are important sources of antioxidants found naturally. They are highest in fresh, raw fruits and vegetables. For optimal health, enjoy five to nine servings per day. In 2004, the United States Department of Agriculture released the following list of foods that contain the highest amounts of antioxidants:[3]

- Artichokes
- Blackberries
- Black beans
- Cranberries
- Cultivated or wild blueberries
- Gala, Granny Smith, or Red Delicious apples
- Pecans
- Pinto beans
- Plums
- Prunes
- Raspberries
- Red kidney beans
- Russet potatoes
- Small red beans

- Strawberries
- Sweet cherries

Most of these foods taste delicious and are not difficult to incorporate into your diet as snacks. Instead of focusing on removing the "bad" foods from your diet, first add a few items from this list. As you add more healthy items, there will be less room for the unhealthier foods. A simple way to start is to try one-quarter cup of fresh berries as a midmorning snack. This high dose of antioxidants with some fiber will keep you going until lunch. Wholesome snacks such as these can be the first of many small choices that will lead you on the path to optimal health. *"So whether you eat or drink, or whatever you do, do it all for the glory of God"* (1 Cor. 10:31 NLT).

The Perils of Processed Foods

Processed foods are fruit, vegetables, grains, and animal products that have been altered mechanically or chemically. For example, a grilled chicken breast and baked potato is an example of a whole-food meal, whereas deep-fried, fast-food chicken nuggets with French fries is not. Although both meals contain the same basic building blocks, the body does not process them the same way. Foods processed by altering their natural state are stripped of nutrients and enzymes that help the body digest the food and absorb them properly.

Eating processed foods can lead to nutritional deficiencies. They have reduced nutritional value and put an added strain on the body by increasing the need for nutrients. An example of this effect is high fructose corn syrup, known as HFCS. Chemically derived from corn, it is one of the most pervasive ingredients in processed foods. It has essentially replaced natural plain sugar in most prepackaged foods. Found in soda, breads, cereal, coffee creamer, ketchup, salad dressings, pasta sauce, and too many other items to list; fructose corn syrup is used widely because it is inexpensive to manufacture, improves taste and texture, is easily mixed into foods, and improves product consistency.

There are health consequences to eating high fructose corn syrup because it is easier to break down and absorb than natural sugar. Foods that contain HFCS are low in fiber and there is nothing to slow down the absorption process. Thus, the molecules are more easily broken down into usable glucose and absorbed into the bloodstream. This quick breakdown leads to a rapid rise in blood sugar. The pancreas responds by quickly releasing high amounts of insulin to bring the blood sugar down to normal, putting undue strain on the pancreas and the insulin receptors that bring glucose into the cells.

Daily repetition of this process continually stimulates insulin production. As the body gets used to higher levels of insulin, the cells stop utilizing it properly. This is a primary factor in insulin resistance or metabolic syndrome, a condition that can lead to type 2 diabetes. In adults, 90 to 95 percent of all diagnosed cases of diabetes are classified as type 2. According to the National Diabetes Information Clearinghouse, the incidence of diagnosed and undiagnosed cases of diabetes in 2007 was estimated at 23.6 million people in the United States alone.[4] The Population Health Metrics released alarming information regarding diabetes in 2010. The study predicts that 1 in 3 Americans will have diabetes by 2050.[5] These figures correlate with the incidence of obesity and the introduction of HFCS into food products. Imagine not having to find the cure to type 2 diabetes by simply removing the cause of the disease instead.

Your Unique Needs

The recommended daily allowance of each nutrient, or RDA, is a helpful guideline for a person's nutritional needs. It was developed by the Food and Nutrition Board of the Institute of Medicine, a nonprofit organization. The RDA for each listed nutrient meets the daily requirements of 97 percent of people. In 1997, the RDA became part of a broader set of recommended nutritional guidelines called the Dietary Reference Intake used by both the United States and Canada.

The other guideline is the recommended daily intake, or RDI, which is used mainly for nutritional labeling. Although most healthy people have the same basic nutritional needs, neither the RDA nor RDI take into account individual variations or an individual's increased or decreased nutrient needs. The amount of nutrients that a person needs can vary due to genetic differences, age, sex, weight, illness, or stress. Just like a snowflake, people look the same from far away; but up close, each person has a distinct pattern that makes him or her unique.

Nutritional Deficiencies

Nutrient deficiencies commonly go unmanaged because their symptoms are subtle and often ignored or dismissed. Few medical practitioners have adequate training or time to review patients' nutrition during office visits. Therefore, each person must make sure his or her nutritional needs are met every day. The best way to ensure you are getting what you need is to eat a variety of foods including fresh fruits and vegetables. Bear in mind that the longer it takes to transport produce across the country to grocery stores, the more nutrients are potentially lost. Buying fresh, local produce and storing it properly preserves precious nutrients. To achieve optimal nutrient levels, supplements can also be helpful. Before taking a supplement, talk to your healthcare provider to ensure it is safe and will not interfere with any medications you are currently taking. Provide a complete list of the supplements you are taking for your healthcare provider to review. Some supplements can affect medication levels and other health conditions.

Certain diseases are due to or can cause nutritional deficiencies. A study in the *Journal of the American Medical Association* confirmed the connection between nutrient deficiencies and many chronic diseases.[6] These diseases include cancer, coronary heart disease, coagulation disorders, and osteoporosis.

A quality multivitamin is a great way to build a strong body. It is preferable to purchase supplements from a health food store rather than a discount retailer because the quality tends to be better. When reading a multivitamin label, make sure it has as wide a range of nutrients as possible. Unless a specific condition requires you to take iron, it is best to take a supplement without it.

Another way to check the quality of a supplement is by reading the "other" or "inactive" ingredients. Avoid supplements that use fillers and binders such as magnesium stearate, lactose, cornstarch, silicon dioxide, titanium dioxide, stearic acid, sodium starch glycolate, talc, sucrose, povidone, pregelatinized starch, hydroxy propyl methylcellulose, Opacode® products (inks and dyes used to label or color tablets), croscarmellose, calcium phosphate, hydroxy propyl cellulose, ethylcellulose, crospovidone, shellac, calcium stearate, sodium benzoate, BHT, BHA, tartrazine (a synthetic yellow dye), peanut oil, hydrogenated cottonseed oil, titanium dioxide, polysorbate 80, red dyes No. 33 and 40, sorbic acid, and fractionated coconut oil.[7] These ingredients are added to allow machines to run faster so companies can save money during production. They are also added to fill empty space in capsules. Regardless of the reason they are included, they are not beneficial and can cause health problems.

People often ask which vitamins are good for certain conditions. Although vitamins are therapeutic for many conditions, don't fool yourself into thinking that any pill, supplement, or vitamin can substitute for poor lifestyle choices. It's easy to say to yourself, "I'm healthy because I take vitamins," but that is not the case. It is vital to eat well—get most of the necessary nutrients from the food you eat—drink enough water, and exercise.

Exercise

The value of physical exercise is not specifically addressed in the Bible. In biblical times, there were no vehicles. People tended to their crops, and manual labor was part of daily life. Jesus and His disciples got exercise by walking to spread the message of the Gospel and healing to those in need. Since physical exercise was a natural part of people's lifestyle, additional exercise was unnecessary. Due to more sedentary modern lifestyles, exercise must be scheduled into daily routines.

Exercise is vital to keep bodies strong, slow the aging process, and protect against disease. Ideally, people should get two hours and 30 minutes per week of moderate exercise, or one hour and 30 minutes of vigorous exercise.[8] Moderate activities include fast walking, cycling, water aerobics, and even gardening. Vigorous activities are running or jogging, swimming laps, or playing sports such as basketball or tennis. This aerobic exercise should be in conjunction with weight training of the larger muscle groups twice weekly.

Though it may be challenging to squeeze exercise into a busy schedule, we cannot live without it. Just as we need eating and sleeping, our bodies require regular exercise. Diseases such as obesity, osteoporosis, heart disease, diabetes, and depression are associated with a sedentary lifestyle. For adequate physical and mental health, we all have to get moving!

So take a new grip with your tired hands and strengthen your weak knees. Mark out a straight path for your feet so that those who are weak and lame will not fall but become strong (Hebrews 12:12-13 NLT).

Practical Tips

Hydrate well. Water is vital to nearly every chemical reaction in our body. It lubricates joints, skin, digestion, and our respiratory system. Very few biochemical reactions in our body do not require water. For maximum health, drink at least eight to ten glasses every day.

> *The Lord will guide you continually, giving you water when you are dry and restoring your strength. You will be like a well-watered garden, like an ever-flowing spring* (Isaiah 58:11 NLT).

Write down what you eat and review your daily intake. It is amazing what happens when you become aware of your habits. You may notice you have been eating much more than you thought. It is also a good idea to chart symptoms such as headaches, indigestion, gas, bloating, constipation, or diarrhea in relation to your intake. This log will help you identify the foods your body does not process well.

Read labels. It is very important to read ingredient lists on packaged foods because many companies attempt to deceive consumers about the health benefits of their products. Challenge yourself to read every label carefully and thoroughly before you put a product in your shopping cart. Avoid purchasing products that contain these: HFCS; preservatives; added salt; added sugars (sucrose, dextrose, maltodextrin, fructose); artificial sweeteners, such as Splenda (sucrolose), NutriSweet, Equal (aspartame), Sweet'N Low (saccharin), and Sunett or Sweet One (acesulfame-K). These artificial sweeteners, which are not part of a healthy diet, are typically found in packaged foods.

Shop the borders. Most grocery stores are designed with whole foods like fruits, vegetables, and meats on the outer perimeter of the store. By purchasing most of your foods from the borders of the store, your diet choices will be more natural. Avoid weaving in and out of the many aisles of prepackaged, preserved, and nutrient-stripped foods. Not only will you eat healthier, but you will also save money and avoid being tempted by packaged convenience foods.

Know your caloric goal. We all come in different sizes and have different goals. Know how many calories your body needs to have enough energy without gaining weight. If you are overweight, consume fewer calories than you burn. Each pound of fat is equivalent to eating an extra 3,500 calories. So that extra five pounds you gained over the holidays is the same as eating 17,500 extra calories. It is amazing how many calories that extra slice of pumpkin pie or glass of eggnog adds to your day's total!

Use the following chart to identify your daily caloric needs:[9]

Dietary Reference Caloric Intakes for Men and Women (age 30)					
Food and Nutrition Board, Institute of Medicine, National Academies					
		MEN[a]		Women[a]	
Height (in)	Activity BMI[b]	18.5 BMI[b]	24.99 BMI[b]	18.5 BMI[b]	24.99 BMI[b]
59	Sedentary	1,848	2,080	1,625	1,762
	Low activity	2,009	2,267	1,803	1,956
	Active	2,215	2,506	2,025	2,198
	Very Active	2,554	2,898	2,291	2,489
65	Sedentary	2,068	2,349	1,816	1,982
	Low activity	2,254	2,566	2,016	2,202
	Active	2,490	2,842	2,267	2,477
	Very Active	2,880	3,296	2,567	2,807
71	Sedentary	2,301	2,635	2,015	2,211
	Low activity	2,513	2,884	2,239	2,459
	Active	2,782	3,200	2,519	2,769

[a]For each year below 30, add 7 calories/day for women and 10 calories/day for men. For each year above 30, subtract 7 calories/day for women and 10 calories/day for men.

BMI[b] = body mass index.

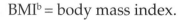

Open the Right Doors

Assess the healthfulness of your lifestyle. Look for open doors where sickness might have entered. Are you eating properly? Are you getting enough sleep? Are you doing what you should do in the natural realm? God does not want us to ignore our physical bodies. We need to respect not only His spiritual laws, but His natural laws as well. Use wisdom with everyday decisions.

Your body is *"the temple of the Holy Spirit"* (1 Cor. 6:19). Take good care of it for optimum health and wellness, and it will serve you well with vitality and strength. Then you, in turn, will be empowered to serve God for many fruitful years like Moses, who *"was one hundred and twenty years old when he died. His eyes were not dim nor his natural vigor diminished"* (Deut. 34:7).

ENDNOTES

1. L.Y. Tomita, A. Longatto Filho, M.C. Costa, M.A. Andreoli, L.L. Villa, E.L. Franco, M.A. Cardoso, "Diet and serum micronutrients in relation to cervical neoplasia and cancer among low-income Brazilian women," *International Journal of Cancer*, February 1, 2010, 126(3):703-14.

2. G. Bobe, J.J. Peterson, G. Gridley, M. Hyer, J.T. Dwyer, L.M. Brown, "Flavonoid consumption and esophageal cancer among black and white men in the United States," *International Journal of Cancer*, September 1, 2009, 125(5):1147-54.

3. Xianli Wu, Gary R. Beecher, Joanne M. Holden, David B. Haytowitz, Susan E. Gebhardt, and Ronald L. Prior , "Lipophilic and Hydrophilic Capacities of Common Foods in the United States," 2004, *Journal of Agricultural and Food Chemistry*, Vol. 52 (12), 4026-4037.

4. National Diabetes Information Clearinghouse, National Institutes of Health of the U.S. Department of Health and Human

Services, *"National Diabetes Statistics,2007,"* NIH Publication No. 08—3892, June 2008, http://diabetes.niddk.nih.gov/dm/pubs/statistics/index.htm#allages.

5. James P. Boyle, Theodore J. Thompson, Edward W. Gregg, Lawrence E. Barker, and David F. Williamson, "Projection of the year 2050 burden of diabetes in the US adult population: dynamic modeling of incidence, mortality, and prediabetes prevalence" Population Health Metrics, October 22, 2010, 8:29doi:10.1186/1478-7954-829.

6. Kathleen M. Fairfield, Robert H. Fletcher, "Vitamins for Chronic Disease Prevention in Adults," *Journal of the American Medical Association,* 2002, 287:3116-3126.

7. U.S. Food and Drug Administration, "Inactive Ingredients Database Download," 2010, http://www.fda.gov/Drugs/InformationOnDrugs/ucm113978.htm.

8. Centers for Disease Control and Prevention, "Physical Activity for Everyone," 2010, http://www.cdc.gov/physicalactivity/everyone/guidelines/adults.html.

9. Panel on Macronutrients, Panel on the Definition of Dietary Fiber, Subcommittee on Upper Reference Levels of Nutrients, Subcommittee on Interpretation and Uses of Dietary Reference Intakes, and the Standing Committee on the Scientific Evaluation of Dietary Reference Intakes, "Dietary Reference Intakes for Energy, Carbohydrate, Fiber, Fat, Fatty Acids, Cholesterol, Protein, and Amino Acids," Food and Nutrition Board, Institute of Medicine, the National Academies, Washington, D.C.: The National Academies Press, 2002.

CHAPTER EIGHT

KEYS TO UNLOCKING FINANCIAL FREEDOM

Disobedience is the deadbolt on the windows of Heaven.

Most people associate the word *prosperity* with wealth, but God wants you to prosper in every way—body, soul, spirit, health, finances, profession, and ministry. The apostle John wrote, *"Beloved, I pray that you may prosper in **all** things and be in health, just as your soul prospers"* (3 John 2). Do not limit your prayers for prosperity to jobs and income alone.

Living in poverty and excessive debt are not part of God's will for your life. God, who richly shares *"all things"* (1 Tim. 6:17) with you, desires that you learn the right way to steward His wealth and riches.

There are keys to prosperity just as there are deadbolts. Once you understand and align your finances with the will and Word of God, you will experience God's blessings.

Prosperity Starts With the Heart

In the Kingdom of God, financial prosperity is linked to the prospering of your soul. Your attitude and approach to receiving and using His wealth begins by acknowledging that everything on this earth—including all that you have—belongs to and comes from His hand. When it was time to build the temple in Jerusalem, King David prayed:

> *Now for the house of my God I have prepared with all my might: gold for things to be made of gold, silver for things of silver, bronze for things of bronze, iron for things of iron, wood for things of wood, onyx stones, stones to be set, glistening stones of various colors, all kinds of precious stones, and marble slabs in abundance. Moreover, because I have set my affection on the house of my God, I have given to the house of my God, over and above all that I have prepared for the holy house, my own special treasure of gold and silver* (1 Chronicles 29:2-3).

David's giving is in accord with the First Commandment—to love the Lord with all his heart, all his soul, and all his strength (see Deut. 6:5). But David took his prayer a step further:

> *...For all that is in heaven and in earth is Yours....Both riches and honor come from You, and You reign over all.... But who am I, and who are my people, that we should be able to offer so willingly as this? For all things come from You, and of Your own we have given You* (1 Chronicles 29:11-12a,14).

David understood that everything he owned belonged to God. He was simply returning a portion of His gifts back to the Giver. Matthew explains how this works in the parable of the talents, a picture of how Jesus gives you money, skills, or gifts and instructs you how to invest in His Kingdom (see Matt. 25:14-30). The key in this parable is your "faithfulness" in how you handle His money and goods. "*...It is required in stewards that one be found faithful*" (1 Cor. 4:2). Jesus asks, "*So if you have not been trustworthy in handling worldly wealth, who will trust you with true riches?*" (Luke 16:11 NIV).

How does the parable of the talents apply to your daily life? It begins with your soul prospering. If your heart is sold out to God, you will be obedient to His voice. When He says to give a certain amount of money to His work or to a stranger you do not know, are you willing and ready to obey? Do you have enough faith in Him to believe He will return more than enough for your needs, or more than you could ever ask or think?

Do you put your faith in your bank account or your paycheck? Is the bank or your job your source? Banks are fallible. The security of your checking account or saving account is not guaranteed. Your paycheck is dependent on long hours keeping your employer satisfied. Neither is your source or your supply.

The more you read and learn about the true source of all life, your confidence will soar. As you feed your stomach, your body functions. As you feed your heart with His Word, your soul prospers.

Your "Trust Account"

Belief in God means you trust Him. You trust in His love. You believe He is a loving and generous Father, and you trust in His faithfulness to provide for all your needs. Even when He disciplines you as a loving Father, His desire is to restore, bless, and make you whole.

Do you believe that? In the ups and downs of living, is your faith in Him constant? Trusting Him opens up your account in Heaven. Knowing He will open His cache of blessings over your life is like withdrawing from your savings account. You know what you have on deposit at the local bank. You should also know what is in your account with Him.

If you find yourself worried about finances and doubting that God will take care of you, confess this unbelief to God. Repent, and watch how your soul prospers. Pray:

Father, I believe. I confess that I have not always trusted in Your love for me. I haven't always believed that You would provide for all my needs and the needs of my family. I confess worry and fear about my finances. I am sorry I don't totally rely on and trust You to take care of me. Take these sins of unbelief, worry, and fear. Put them on the cross. Wash me and cleanse me of these sins. I declare that You will provide for all my needs according to Your riches in glory in Christ Jesus. Thank You, Jesus.

Garbage In, Garbage Out

How are you feeding your soul? What is shaping your view of the world and the economy—the news or the Word of God? *"...Faith comes by hearing, and hearing by the word of God"* (Rom. 10:17). Fear and worry come by hearing the news and the barrage of negativism from the media and other influences around you. What you listen to will affect your soul, your heart, and your mind. If you listen to the unbelief, the heresy, the hate, and the anger of the world, is it any wonder that you doubt the precious things of God?

The world's system teaches the opposite of God's Word. Recession, depression, foreclosures, unemployment, and failure are not in God's plan for your life. Talking about negatives will not encourage or edify. Avoid feeding your soul or your environment with garbage.

Jesus told His disciples:

Therefore do not worry, saying, "What shall we eat?" or "What shall we drink?" or "What shall we wear?" For after all these things the Gentiles seek. For your heavenly Father knows that

you need all these things. But seek first the kingdom of God and His righteousness, and all these things shall be added to you (Matthew 6:31-33).

Do not allow fear to enter your life. Feed yourself with the fruit of the Spirit: love, joy, peace, compassion, and faith (see Gal. 5:22-23; Eph. 5:9).

God knows when even one sparrow falls from the sky. He says you are more valuable than a sparrow (see Matt. 10:31). In the future, your faith in Him and His provisions will be just one example of His incredible wealth, favor, and kindness toward you and your family. *"That in the ages to come He might show the exceeding riches of His grace in His kindness toward us in Christ Jesus"* (Eph. 2:7).

Even in these difficult economic times, align yourself with the Word of God. Let your life become a testimony to His supernatural provision:

Enlarge the place of your tent, and let them stretch out the curtains of your dwellings; do not spare; lengthen your cords, and strengthen your stakes. For you shall expand to the right and to the left... (Isaiah 54:2-3).

Overcome by Faith

Regardless of your circumstances and even if the world is going through a recession, proclaim God's Word and His promises over yourself, your family, and your finances: *"For all the promises of God in Him are Yes, and in Him Amen, to the glory of God through us"* (2 Cor. 1:20). Prophesy over yourself, "Everything I put my hand to shall prosper" (see Ps. 1:3) and *"...my God shall supply all* [my] *need according to His riches in glory by Christ Jesus"* (Phil. 4:19).

This is the hour for believers to be signs and wonders (see Isa. 8:18) to the people in the world who are fearful and without hope in an unstable economy. God's people will be examples that He can supply all their needs, including comfortable homes and nice cars.

God wants you to have nice things as long as the nice things don't have you—and you give generously to God. Start praying and believing God to write tithe checks for $1 million. If you say, "Obviously, she doesn't know how much I make," you just cut off your blessing. God's blessing does not depend on how much you earn. Ask Him to speak to you and show you how much to give. When you obey, He will bless you mightily. Live with His faith filling your heart and allow it to affect every choice you make.

Give, and it will be given to you: good measure, pressed down, shaken together, and running over will be put into your bosom. For with the same measure that you use, it will be measured back to you (Luke 6:38).

Get Rid of the Poverty Mindset

Despite God's mindset of blessing, many people—even those who have been set free from the spirit of poverty—are still holding on to a mindset of poverty. "I can't afford it," is the first thing out of their mouths. Don't put a word curse on your finances. Instead, be careful what you confess because negative words block financial prosperity. Remember God's abundant blessings and begin trusting Him.

Trust in the Lord with all your heart, and lean not on your own understanding; in all your ways acknowledge Him, and He shall direct your paths (Proverbs 3:5-6).

Lay hands on your checkbook and prophesy the Word of God over your job and sources of income. Be specific when you pray. For example, say, "Thank You for bringing in more money," or "Thank You for bringing in 20 percent more than last year." Write down what you owe and pray with faith for the payment of all your debts.

Do not accept the lie that God wants to humble you through poverty. *"Let no one cheat you of your reward, taking delight in false humility..."* (Col. 2:18). But rather, *"...say continually, 'Let the Lord be magnified, who has pleasure in the prosperity of His servant'"* (Ps. 35:27).

Blocks to Financial Freedom

Disobedience is the deadbolt on the windows of Heaven— and repentance and obedience are the keys to open those same windows. Despite God's intention to prosper you, sin can block your blessings. *"He who covers his sins will not prosper, but whoever confesses and forsakes them will have mercy"* (Prov. 28:13).

If you believe your finances could improve, examine your heart for these hindrances to financial blessing:

1. Foolish spending.

2. Withholding the tithe.

3. Disobedience to what God tells you to give as offerings.

Foolish Spending

Check your "foolish spending temperature" with an examination of your credit card debt. Credit card offers are not income. They are roads to greater debt. Pray for wisdom and discernment in your investing and spending habits.

However, not all debt is foolish spending. Housing, food, and transportation are genuine needs, and most people have to borrow money for mortgages and car payments. Foolish spending is living beyond your means. Ask God to help you discern the difference between your needs and wants, between His blessing and self-indulgence.

When you repent of foolish spending, you acknowledge that everything you own really belongs to God. Are you being a faithful steward of His wealth? Understanding that all money belongs to Him actually takes pressure off you. He is Your source. Your provision is His responsibility. You do not have to worry about it. He will tell you where to go and what to do to open the supply. All you must do is be faithful and obedient.

Prayer for Foolish Spending

Father, forgive me for not wisely stewarding all You have given me. I repent for spending what You gave me on things I don't need. Take this sin from me now. I choose to spend money as You lead, to give to others as You lead, and to save the money You tell me to save. Thank You, Jesus.

Tithes and Offerings

"Bring all the tithes into the storehouse, that there may be food in My house, and try Me now in this," says the Lord of hosts, "If I will not open for you the windows of heaven and pour out for you such blessing that there will not be room enough to receive it" (Malachi 3:10).

When times get tight, some people cut back on tithes and offerings. Some even stop attending church to lower their car expenses. That choice will cut off your blessings. If you want to cut your spending, why not do without your daily specialty coffee?

Trusting in God is a key to tithing with the right attitude—and receiving the right results: blessings. The stingy servant who hoarded his master's wealth, told his master:

*"Lord, I knew you to be a hard man, reaping where you have not sown, and gathering where you have not scattered seed."
... But his lord answered and said to him, "You wicked and lazy servant, you knew that I reap where I have not sown, and gather where I have not scattered seed. So you ought to have deposited my money with the bankers, and at my coming I would have received back my own with interest. Therefore take the talent from him, and give it to him who has ten talents. For to everyone who has, more will be given, and he will have abundance; but from him who does not have, even what he has will be taken away. And cast the unprofitable servant into the outer darkness. There will be weeping and gnashing of teeth"* (Matthew 25:24;26-30).

The master blessed and prospered the two servants who had been faithful with their master's wealth. He told each:

..."Well done, good and faithful servant; you were faithful over a few things, I will make you ruler over many things. Enter into the joy of your lord" (Matthew 25:21,23).

Disobedience

If God tells you to give an offering, ask Him what He wants you to give. He may ask you for something you believe you cannot afford. Disobedience will hinder your financial blessings. In Second Chronicles 24:20, the Holy Spirit fell on Zechariah and he prophesied: *"Thus says God: 'Why do you transgress the commandments of the Lord, so that you cannot prosper?'"*

If He asks you for something unique, He has something even better in mind to bless you. He will provide the seed for the sower (see 2 Cor. 9:10). He will provide you with finances, food, clothes, homes, cars, and other needs of life. Be sensitive to

His voice. He may give you something so you can bless someone else in His name.

Do You Want to Be a River or a Reservoir?

God wants His people to be a river of His finances, not a reservoir to hoard His blessings. Remember, rivers have "banks"! His guidance will direct your "river" to the person, ministry, or situation where His blessings can do the most good.

As you give freely and obediently, God continues to cause His blessings to rain on your life. He is not limited by the average percentage rate of return set by the government banking system. He doesn't increase or decrease His blessings based on the world's economy. Investing in God is always a good thing, not a shady underhanded deal that promises a fast return. God always blesses those who bless Him. He always keeps His promises.

God's return on your investment is going to outstrip any bank's interest rates.

After my divorce, I lost everything, including my home. I moved into a smaller home with my girls. My salary compared to my cost of living should have resulted in a negative balance at the end of each month. Nevertheless, I continued tithing off the gross of all my income. My CPA told me to stop tithing and giving offerings and to declare bankruptcy. I said, "I cut those words off from my life, in Jesus' name," and I got a new CPA. I aligned my finances with the Word of God, and God made up the difference. I had money left at the end of the month instead of a month left without money. God miraculously provided for all our needs.

He will provide for yours, too. He *"gives you power to get wealth"* (Deut. 8:18)—it may not always be a direct deposit from Heaven—although that can happen, too!

Align Your Finances With the Word of God

Once you get your finances lined up with God's Word, you will be blessed. He knows you will use your finances to open the windows of Heaven. This begins by humbling yourself before God, both corporately and individually:

If My people who are called by My name will humble themselves, and pray and seek My face, and turn from their wicked ways, then I will hear from heaven, and will forgive their sin and heal their land (2 Chronicles 7:14).

The *"wicked ways"* in this verse can refer to any form of sin. Break open that deadbolt of disobedience. When you pray over your finances, begin by humbling yourself before God and repenting of any sins. Then take authority over any hindrances, as the Holy Spirit leads you, and thank God for His provision and blessing. Prophesy the Word of God over your finances. Be specific: "A new client will call today." "A check will come in the mail today." Pray: "Thank You, Jesus, for supplying all my needs today and paying off this bill, buying me a new laptop, supplying my children's tuition." Thank Him for His provision both *before* you receive it and *after* He sends it to you.

Prayers to Open the Deadbolt:
A General Prayer

Father, I repent for _____ (foolish spending, failing to tithe regularly, disobedience in giving the offerings You have asked of me). That is sin. Take it from me now and put it on the cross of Jesus Christ, never to be held against me again, in Jesus' name. Thank You, Jesus. Help me to be wise and faithful in my spending. Help me to be faithful to tithe and give offerings according to Your will. Give me discernment so I can sow in good soil that will produce fruit for Your Kingdom. Let me

hear the voice of Your Holy Spirit about how much to give and who to give to. Thank You, Jesus.

Prayer of Repentance for Unfaithfulness in Tithes and Offerings

Father, I have not been faithful and consistent in my tithe. This is sin. Forgive me of this sin and put it on the cross, never to be held against me again. And Jesus, thank You for the promise in Your Word that says:

Honor the Lord with your possessions, and with the firstfruits of all your increase; so your barns will be filled with plenty, and your vats will overflow with new wine (Proverbs 3:9-10).

And Father, when You told me to give an offering of _____ to _____, I disobeyed You. Forgive me for my disobedience and for my unbelief in Your faithful provision. Put these sins on the cross of Jesus, never to be held against me again. Help me hear Your voice so I can always be obedient to give tithes and offerings according to Your will.

Prayer Over an Offering

Father, thank You that this seed I am planting in good soil will come up quickly and bear fruit. Thank You for supplying for all my needs so I can continue to sow into Your Kingdom. I thank You for my_____ (pay raise, bonus, donations, job). I break all hindrances against this, in Jesus' name. Bless anyone who owes me money and thank You for moving on their hearts that they will repay it soon, in Jesus' name. Amen.

PART IV

TO THE 4 CORNERS OF YOUR WORLD

CHAPTER NINE

ANOINTED TO HEAL!

Before Aaron ministered as high priest, Moses *"poured some of the anointing oil on Aaron's head and anointed him, to consecrate him"* (Lev. 8:12). The anointing oil, a symbol of the Holy Spirit, was a sign of God's approval of Aaron for divine service.

Christ means "anointed"[1] in New Testament Greek. Likewise, the Hebrew equivalent "Messiah" is derived from the Hebrew word for anointed.If you have received Jesus Christ as Savior, then the anointed One lives in you. He also lives in you through the Holy Spirit, who is available to all. *"How much more will your heavenly Father give the Holy Spirit to those who ask Him"* (Luke 11:13b).

Just as Aaron was anointed to consecrate him and make him holy, God desires to anoint and purify you. This requires that you receive all that He has for you and surrender to how and when He wishes to use you.

His anointing is not meant for you—it is for others. Its purpose is not to make you look good. God's anointing is meant to move through you to touch others. You no longer live for yourself. You choose willingly to lay down your life for Him and for His ministry. That precious anointing helps you fulfill God's will for your life as you pour yourself out for others.

How Do You Know
What God Wants You to Do?

To walk in His anointing, you must be available to God and be sensitive to His will for your life. When you are in a right relationship with Him, your anointing will increase whether you minister from the pulpit, one on one, or in the privacy of your home.

Spend quality, intimate time with God every day. Set aside a time to seek Him and to wait on Him. *"...Seek the Lord your God, and you will find Him if you seek Him with all your heart and with all your soul"* (Deut. 4:29).

Talk to God: "What is Your perfect will for my life, Father? I lay all my dreams and visions on Your altar. If they are from You, they will come to pass in Your perfect timing. I want to follow Your direction. Speak to me." Then be still and listen for His voice. Jesus said, *"My sheep hear My voice"* (John 10:27a).

Just like you schedule your meals, work, or bedtime, you must also schedule time for God on a regular basis. If you work full time, spend time with Him early in the morning, during your lunch break, or before you go to bed at night. It is important to get alone with God away from the confusing distractions of the world. Occasionally, take a day or two away for a retreat with Him. Jacob was by himself when he had an encounter with God:

> *Then Jacob was left alone; and a Man wrestled with him until the breaking of day. ... Then Jacob asked, saying, "Tell me Your name, I pray." And He said, "Why is it that you ask about My name?" And He blessed him there. So Jacob called the name of the place Peniel: "For I have seen God face to face, and my life is preserved"* (Genesis 32:24;29-30).

Practice listening for His voice. Expect to hear His quiet whispers. He cares about every area of your life and will tell you what to do next when you are open and listening for His direction.

A Time of Preparation

God desires to use each of His children. Paul encouraged the Corinthian church, *"Whenever you come together, each of you has a psalm, has a teaching, has a tongue, has a revelation, has an interpretation"* (1 Cor. 14:26b). In his Epistle to the Ephesians, Paul explained that believers will grow in their calling *"according to the effective working by which every part does its share"* (Eph. 4:16). You have an important part to play in God's master design.

Whether you desire a deeper walk with Him or have a call on your life to fivefold ministry, never move ahead of God. When the Lord told Moses in the wilderness, *"My Presence will go with you, and I will give you rest,"* Moses answered, *"If Your Presence does not go with us, do not bring us up from here"* (Exod. 33:14-15).

Many well-intentioned people have stepped out in ministry before God's timing and have ended up hurt and disillusioned. They were not fully prepared and ran ahead of God. God can give you a dream, but that seed may have to germinate and grow before you are mature enough to move forward. When your dreams and visions don't manifest immediately, it's tempting to get impatient or discouraged, not realizing that He is carefully preparing you for His call on your life. Remember, *"He who calls you is faithful, who also will do it"* (1 Thess. 5:24). Luke 1:45 says, *"Blessed is she who believed, for there will be a fulfillment of those things which were told her from the Lord."*

As a young man, Joseph had visions of what his future held. His brothers laughed. Years later, his vision became a reality. David was anointed king of Israel many years before the crown was placed on his head. Both young men had to go through numerous difficulties and trials before God could use them in His perfect plan.

Before Esther was presented to the king, she went through a year of preparation.

Each young woman's turn came to go in to King Ahasuerus after she had completed twelve months' preparation, according to the regulations for the women, for thus were the days of their preparation apportioned: six months with oil of myrrh, and six months with perfumes and preparations for beautifying women (Esther 2:12).

Before God can use you for His purposes, you must willingly study, wait, and prepare. If God doesn't give you specific directions immediately, be faithful where you are. Moses waited 40 years tending sheep in the wilderness (see Acts 7:29-34). Paul's prelude to his ministry lasted more than three years (see Gal. 1:15-18).

Even Jesus had years of preparation before He could step into His ministry at age 30. After His baptism by John, the Holy Spirit led Him into the desert for 40 days and nights where the devil tempted and tested Him. Once He was fully prepared, He came out of the wilderness to begin His ministry (see Matt. 4:1-11).

Waiting on the Lord is not a passive activity like waiting for a bus. Moses, Esther, David, Joseph, and Paul went through an active time of preparation and testing during which the Lord honed, polished, and prepared them for service.

The Word promises that as you wait on the Lord, you will renew your strength; you will *"mount up with wings like eagles"*; you will *"run and not be weary...walk and not faint"* (Isa. 40:31).

You must prepare yourself to be used in His Kingdom. During that time of preparation, soak in the anointing of His presence. Study His Word. Listen to good teachers. Reach out to those God brings along your path. No one starts a world-wide ministry the first week or the first year. As God trusts your obedience to minister to your neighbor, He can lead you to the next person. As you teach your own child, He may open the door for you to teach a class at church.

Be faithful and open to learning and practicing His will. Just as you had to pass one grade in school before you could advance to the next, you will also graduate from one level to the next in God's school of ministry. Sometimes you may have to repeat a grade if you do not catch the intention or meaning of the test God has set before you. Remember, His people had to go around the mountain many times before they were prepared to walk into and claim the Promised Land.

Consecration Precedes Being Sent

When there seems to be a delay in your progress, ask God to show you the cause. There may be sin in your life He wants you to deal with. When God called Isaiah to the prophetic ministry, Isaiah said:

> …"Woe is me, for I am undone! Because I am a man of unclean lips, and I dwell in the midst of a people of unclean lips; for my eyes have seen the King, the Lord of hosts." Then one of the seraphim flew to me, having in his hand a live coal which he had taken with the tongs from the altar. And he touched my mouth with it, and said: "Behold, this has touched your lips; your iniquity is taken away, and your sin purged." Also I heard the voice of the Lord, saying: "Whom shall I send, and who will go for Us?" Then I said, "Here am I! Send me" (Isaiah 6:5-8).

He may want you to do other things or meet other people before He opens those ministry doors. Know that He brings people across your path to prepare you before He gives you more responsibility.

Moses' testing in the desert resulted in a character change. After 40 years tending sheep, he was transformed from a somewhat prideful young man who couldn't understand why his people didn't immediately acknowledge his role as a leader, to the most humble man on the face of the earth (see Acts 7:25; Num. 12:3).

Moses was filled with the anointing for his calling after many years of consecration. The man who came out of the wilderness ready to serve God was not the same man who entered. Moses was a changed man. He was prepared to listen and obey God's voice.

Be Willing to Change—
Without Change We Wouldn't Have Butterflies

God is in the people-changing business. He wants to fill you up with His life and anointing until there is no room left for self. He wants you *"to know the love of Christ which passes knowledge; that you may be filled with all the fullness of God"* (Eph. 3:19). As He pours out His new wine, you must be like a new wineskin. Are you willing to be flexible enough to hold the new wine of the anointing?

> *And no one puts new wine into old wineskins; or else the new wine bursts the wineskins, the wine is spilled, and the wineskins are ruined. But new wine must be put into new wineskins* (Mark 2:22).

Allow God to hone the rough places of your character and correct your attitudes so He can use you. This divine process requires you to:

> *...Let the Spirit renew your thoughts and attitudes. Put on your new nature, created to be like God—truly righteous and holy* (Ephesians 4:23-24 NLT).

As you surrender to God's desires, you will see the fruit of positive change in your life:

Then we will no longer be immature like children. We won't be tossed and blown about by every wind of new teaching. We will not be influenced when people try to trick us with lies so clever they sound like the truth. Instead, we will speak the truth in love, growing in every way more and more like Christ, who is the head of His body, the church. He makes the whole body fit together perfectly. As each part does its own special work, it helps the other parts grow, so that the whole body is healthy and growing and full of love (Ephesians 4:14-16 NLT).

Sometimes you need to change not only how you think but also how you act. When I was traveling with my parents on ministry trips, I was responsible for the announcements, the book table, and the finances. As they got older, they started handing me the microphone to pray for people—and the people were healed. I was doing what I was destined to do without promotion or recognition. I was willing to do whatever was needed.

You may be called to work under a mentor to experience both the challenges of ministry as well as the submission of a true servant. You may have to wear whatever hat it takes to get the job done—with or without accolades. All God's kids have their part in the worldwide puzzle put together piece by piece, person by person, to create His perfect masterpiece. As part of the team, I still travel the world, lay hands on the sick, vacuum floors, clean toilets, and take out the trash. Ministry is 24/7, 365 days a year. Jesus said:

For who is greater, he who sits at the table, or he who serves? Is it not he who sits at the table? Yet I am among you as the One who serves (Luke 22:27).

Count the Cost

Many people want to be in ministry, but how many are willing to pay the price? What if God wants you to give up your home, your family, or your lifestyle? Are you willing to give up your dreams or the most precious thing you own? Are you willing to give up your life if He asks? Are you willing to be misunderstood and criticized for Him?

In Mark 14:3-4, a woman broke an alabaster flask over Jesus' head. Some people became indignant and called her action a waste of money. Yet this woman gave Jesus all she had regardless of the cost. She willingly gave without reservation. She loved Jesus so much, she simply gave Him everything.

What does God want? You. Jesus wants your whole heart, your time, your finances, your mind, and your body. He wants everything.

God never said it would be easy. He never promised life would be painless and easy. However, He did say you would make it *through* the valley of the shadow of death (see Ps. 23:4). When the time came for Esther to fulfill her destiny, she hesitated because she didn't want to risk her life by appearing before the king without being summoned. Her uncle Mordecai exhorted her:

> *For if you remain completely silent at this time, relief and deliverance will arise for the Jews from another place, but you and your father's house will perish. Yet who knows whether you have come to the kingdom for such a time as this?* (Esther 4:14)

Esther became willing to give her all to God, even if it meant sacrificing her life. There are many who have given their lives to Him for ministry and as martyrs through the centuries. Are you willing to give your all?

Set Your Face Like Flint

Giving your all to God means living as a disciple and picking up your cross daily to follow Him. It may mean going to a country where you are expected to eat monkey brains, sleep on a rock with bugs crawling around you, and wash your clothes in a river. It may mean spending quality time with someone you would rather avoid. You may have to give up your beauty sleep, cosmetics, fancy clothes, and regular showers. Instead of a nice comfortable car to drive, you may be very grateful to share a cart with chickens or pigs as you bump down a trail to your next destination.

Regardless of what appears around you or what the voices of the world have to say, you have to make a quality decision to serve Him and be obedient to Him. You will be representing Him to everyone you meet, talk to, or touch. You may be the only "Jesus with skin on" that another person will ever hear from or touch.

Not only are you giving up your personal wants, but often your decision directly affects those you love, your earthly family. It is not an easy decision to make. Make sure you have heard from God. When you are certain you are in His will, allow Him to take care of all the details. He will open the necessary doors. When you put Him first, He will tell you what to do and where to go. When you take care of Him and His work, He will take care of you.

The Holy Spirit, speaking about Jesus through Isaiah's words, said:

For the Lord God will help Me; therefore I will not be disgraced; therefore I have set My face like a flint, and I know that I will not be ashamed (Isaiah 50:7).

Personally, I want to accomplish everything God has appointed for me to do on the earth. I don't want to get in the way of God's call. I want to be like Joshua, who said:

*And if it seems evil to you to serve the Lord, choose for your-
selves this day whom you will serve, whether the gods which
your fathers served that were on the other side of the River, or
the gods of the Amorites, in whose land you dwell. But as for
me and my house, we will serve the Lord* (Joshua 24:15).

Dealing With Adversity

When opposition or adverse situations arise, do not quit or
get discouraged. You must press on. You must continue doing
what God has directed. When you meet resistance, go to Him
first. Ask God, "Why? Did I do anything or overlook something
to cause this situation?" Listen to His voice. You may have done
nothing wrong and God may be ready to overturn the opposition just as He did in Joseph's life. Joseph told his brothers, "...
*you meant evil against me; but God meant it for good, in order to bring
it about as it is this day, to save many people alive"* (Gen. 50:20).

When Moses and the children of Israel left Egypt, they were
certainly in God's perfect will. However, when they had Pha-
raoh's army behind them and the Red Sea blocking their way
to freedom, Moses may have thought he had missed God. They
all were in the right place at the right time for God to perform a
mighty miracle and show everyone His power and faithfulness
to His promises.

When adversity raises its ugly head, first examine yourself. If God doesn't reveal something you have to take care of
in your own life, believe He has something great coming just
around the corner. As you walk in His anointing and follow His
voice, He may make you the Moses in your world. The enemy
always seems to attack just before a breakthrough or a miracle
manifests. Expect God to work mightily in your situation and
walk across a dry riverbed into your promised land.

Be a thermostat, not a thermometer. When you walk into a
room, set the precedent and have everyone else rise to the

standard of a godly and loving environment. Don't react to opposition or belligerence or put up with backbiting. Don't listen to people who tell you to give up. Raise your shield of faith if they try to drag you down or discourage your progress. God called you—not people. You are called to love and serve others, not to worry about or fear what they say. *"...Perfect love casts out fear..."* (1 John 4:18).

As a mature believer, you know the enemy is waiting for an area to attack and stop God's work. Often those attacks come through well-meaning friends, family, or ministers. Listen and know you are hearing from God. Look for confirmation through His Word. Seek godly counsel from those whom you trust. Pray in agreement with His Word. Sometimes you have to wait for God to work out the details, fight the battle for you, and clear the adversity from your path.

Paul declared, *"And we know that all things work together for good to those who love God, to those who are the called according to His purpose"* (Rom. 8:28).

In committing to God's will, be as immovable and steadfast as flint. God who has called you will also anoint you. *"He who calls you is faithful, who also will do it"* (1 Thess. 5:24).

Be Faithful in Finances

Just as a wise, loving parent would not assign an adult task to an unprepared child or adolescent, God expects you to mature spiritually before He sends you out to minister. Spiritual maturity has nothing to do with your age. Whether you are 15, 40, or 80 years of age, spiritual maturity is a matter of the heart, mind, and spirit.

God will test you in the area of finances. Why? What do finances have to do with going to the 4 corners of the earth, laying hands on people, and seeing them healed? Jesus makes it clear that money itself is not the issue. Rather, do you use money with integrity and faithfulness to Him and His purposes?

He who is faithful in what is least is faithful also in much; and he who is unjust in what is least is unjust also in much. Therefore if you have not been faithful in the unrighteous mammon, who will commit to your trust the true riches? And if you have not been faithful in what is another man's, who will give you what is your own? No servant can serve two masters; for either he will hate the one and love the other, or else he will be loyal to the one and despise the other. You cannot serve God and mammon (Luke 16:10-13).

Faithfulness in tithes, offerings, and finances in general not only releases personal financial prosperity, but it is also a key to becoming a vessel of His anointing:

Honor the Lord with your possessions, and with the firstfruits of all your increase; so your barns will be filled with plenty, and your vats will overflow with new wine (Proverbs 3:9-10).

New Wine

Remember, new wine is a symbol of the anointing of the Holy Spirit. On the Day of Pentecost, when the disciples were filled with the Holy Spirit and spoke in tongues:

So they were all amazed and perplexed, saying to one another, "Whatever could this mean?" Others mocking said, "They are full of new wine." But Peter...said to them, "... these are not drunk, as you suppose, since it is only the third hour of the day. But this is what was spoken by the prophet Joel: 'And it shall come to pass in the last days, says God, that I will pour out of My Spirit on all flesh; your sons and your daughters shall prophesy, your young men shall see visions, your old men shall dream dreams. And on My menservants and on My maidservants I will pour out My Spirit in those days; and they shall prophesy'" (Acts 2:12-18).

God is still filling His disciples today with new wine, the anointing of the Holy Spirit. All we have to do is ask.

So I say to you, ask, and it will be given to you; seek, and you will find; knock, and it will be opened to you. For everyone who asks receives, and he who seeks finds, and to him who knocks it will be opened. If a son asks for bread from any father among you, will he give him a stone? Or if he asks for a fish, will he give him a serpent instead of a fish? Or if he asks for an egg, will he offer him a scorpion? If you then, being evil, know how to give good gifts to your children, how much more will your heavenly Father give the Holy Spirit to those who ask Him!" (Luke 11:9-13)

Each of us has different gifts and callings, but there is an abundance of anointing for every vessel. Esther 1:7-8 is a picture of this truth:

And they served drinks in golden vessels, each vessel being different from the other, with royal wine in abundance, according to the generosity of the king. In accordance with the law, the drinking was not compulsory; for so the king had ordered all the officers of his household, that they should do according to each man's pleasure.

What the Anointing Is Not

You may hear many definitions of the anointing, what it does, what it feels like, its attributes, how you get it, and how you keep it. I have talked about what it is. Because there are many false notions about God's precious anointing, I am going to explain what it is not.

First, His anointing does not depend on your physical age, academic or Bible school degrees, or number of years since salvation. There is no scriptural basis for being good enough or not good enough—God decides who will be used and blessed with the anointing to accomplish His work.

When you are ready and willing, He will put people in your path who have a need. He will depend on you to reach out and pray for the hurting and sick. As you listen to His voice, obey His direction, and move out in faith to minister, He will anoint you for success. Keep in mind, the actual healing is God's responsibility. Your responsibility is to be available, to be willing to be led by Him, and to pray for those He brings to you.

God's anointing doesn't depend on your emotional or physical state. You don't need to *feel* the anointing. People will be healed when you pray for them whether you feel anything or not, or whether you are tired or under the weather. Everything depends on Jesus, who lives in you. Healing was a way of life for Him, and it should be a way of life for you as well.

After a service, I was packing up the book table when I noticed a woman ministering to a person at the front of the church. She backed up about five feet, returned to the person and went spit, spit, spit on her. If anyone ministers to others after one of my services ends, people assume that person is part of my ministry team. This woman was not with me and did not have permission to minister. As I watched and wondered what she was doing, she backed up again, returned, and went spit, spit, spit again. I approached her and said, "Excuse me, what are you doing?"

She said, "I am mustering up the anointing."

I explained, "You don't need to muster up the anointing. You *walk* in the anointing."

She replied, "Well then, you do it."

I discerned that she needed deliverance and knew she should not be laying hands on anyone. The woman she wanted to pray for had three incurable diseases. I prayed for the other woman, and within five minutes, all the pain and outward manifestations of her diseases were gone—without mustard, ketchup, or spit.

You cannot generate the anointing any more than you can generate the electricity in the wall. It is simply there. Plug into it, flip the switch, and let it flow. You don't need to add anything to the anointing. Every believer is called to lay hands on the sick, see people recover, and cast out devils without screaming, special effects, or spitting.

You need to know that you know that you walk in His anointing. You don't have to muster it up. Some have the anointing to teach, some to sing, and some to preach. God gives you the anointing you need at the time you need it for the present situation. Don't try to work up the anointing. Walk in it!

The 4 Corners of Your World

God wants to equip believers to take His healing power beyond the 4 walls of the church to the 4 corners of the earth. You may not be the one called to go to India or to travel the world. However, your 4 corners of the earth are actually the 4 corners of *your* world—your family, your neighborhood, where you shop and work. Whether or not it is your calling to take the healing power of God around the globe, it is your job to take it with you wherever you go.

When the time of your release into ministry is at hand, you may discover the answer you have been seeking is right around the corner. If you pray, "Father, send me around the world," He may answer, "Go to your neighbor."

"I'll go anywhere You want me to go, Lord. I'll do anything You want me to do."

God says, "Go pray for your neighbor."

"Father, I'll go anywhere according to Your will, not mine."

God says, "Go visit your brother."

"Send me to the mission field."

God says, "Go to the supermarket."

"I'll go, but I need more anointing. I need more finances."

God asks, "What are you doing with what I've already given to you?"

Have you been faithful with what God has already given you? Have you been faithful with your tithes and offerings? Have you been obedient to what He has already laid on your heart? Why would He send you around the world, if you have not been faithful to go across the street? Have you obeyed His voice in everything He has asked you to do? The anointing starts by hearing His voice and responding, "Yes, Lord."

Use the anointing you have. As you release it to others, your anointing will increase. The rule of giving and receiving is not limited to finances. As you give His anointing, you will receive more in return. As you reach out to heal a person's illness or pain, yours just may disappear also. You pray with His anointing to bless another's finances, and yours will prosper.

When the Time Is at Hand

When God is ready to fulfill the dreams and visions He has given you, there will be no more delay. The time will be ripe for you to walk in His anointing.

When God was ready to fulfill a word He had given to Ezekiel, He told the prophet:

> "...the house of Israel is saying, 'The vision that he sees is for many days from now, and he prophesies of times far off.'

Therefore say to them, 'Thus says the Lord God: "None of My words will be postponed any more, but the word which I speak will be done," says the Lord God'" (Ezekiel 12:27-28).

God told the prophet Habakkuk:

For the vision is yet for an appointed time; but at the end it will speak, and it will not lie. Though it tarries, wait for it; because it will surely come. It will not tarry (Habakkuk 2:3).

As you walk with God, you will receive all that He has for you in His perfect timing. David said, *"But as for me, I trust in You, O Lord; I say, 'You are my God.' My times are in Your hand"* (Ps. 31:14-15a). When He is ready to send you, you will see God move in a miraculous way. You will operate in the gifts of the Spirit, heal the sick in Jesus' name, and minister to people with words of knowledge. You will be trained, equipped, and on fire for God. Be willing to do whatever He wants you to do and go wherever He wants you to go, no matter what the cost.

God desires to do signs and wonders through you. Pray, as the believers did in Acts 4:29-30, that He will:

...grant to Your servants that with all boldness they may speak Your word, by stretching out Your hand to heal, and that signs and wonders may be done through the name of Your holy Servant Jesus.

Amen.

ENDNOTE

1. From Strong's Concordance In the Greek #5547 Christos means anointed. #4899 in Hebrew Messiah means anointed one.

CHAPTER TEN

STEPS TO PRAY FOR HEALING

Now a certain man was there who had an infirmity thirty-eight years. When Jesus saw him lying there, and knew that he already had been in that condition a long time, He said to him, "Do you want to be made well?" (John 5:5-6)

How do you approach someone who needs healing? How do you open the door? What do you say?

Many of us walk up to someone in a mall or a grocery store and simply say, "God sent me here today to pray for you. Is there anything that I can pray with you about?"

No matter where you are, God will put people in your path who need prayer, whether you are in a restroom, a store, or on an airplane. You can pray for someone on the phone, at church, or at a family reunion. Even if you are housebound and cannot travel around the world to minister, God will send somebody to your door or a wrong number on the telephone who needs a word from Him *"The Lord directs the steps of the godly. He delights in every detail of their lives"* (Ps. 37:23 NLT).

It's not sacrilegious to pray for someone in a restroom or anywhere else, for that matter. Once when my mother was in a ladies' room, she overheard a woman in the stall next to her complaining about severe menstrual cramps. When the woman came out of the stall, my mom was waiting there to pray for her. The woman was healed instantly. You never know where or when God will send people to you for ministry.

The apostle Paul exhorts us to be ready at all times, 24/7, *"in season and out of season"* (2 Tim. 4:2a). When you say, "God sent me here to pray for you. Is there anything I can pray for you about?" the person may cry and say, "I got up this morning and prayed, 'God, if You're real, send somebody here to tell me.'" You're it. You are God in the flesh to that person.

Man's theology, his natural thinking, has made healing hard. But healing is actually easy. Jesus laid hands on the sick and they were healed. Healing is also logical. If a person has cancer, curse the cancer and the prions, in Jesus' name. If someone has a headache, lay hands on his or her head. If a person's neck hurts, place your hand where it hurts and pray. When you pray for yourself, lay hands on the area where the pain or problem is.

Remember, don't take on the responsibility for the healing. It's God's responsibility to heal—yours is to pray. Relying on Him and not on yourself will set you free to minister healing without reservations or hesitation.

Once you accept that *He* is the Healer and that *you* are simply available to pray as you are led and anointed by His Holy Spirit, the following nine steps should help guide you as you minister healing to others.

1. Ask.

When you approach someone, begin by asking, "What do you need Jesus to do for you?" Don't assume you know what that person is believing for or needs. Jesus often approached people with a question. When He left Jericho, two blind men sitting by the side of the road called out to Him.

So Jesus stood still and called them, and said, "What do you want Me to do for you?" They said to Him, "Lord, that our eyes may be opened." So Jesus had compassion and touched their eyes. And immediately their eyes received sight, and they followed Him (Matthew 20:32-34).

2. Look.

Maintain eye contact with those you are praying for. It is very important that you keep your eyes open to monitor what is happening to the person receiving prayer. If your eyes are closed and the Holy Spirit touches the person, he or she might fall and hurt him or herself or someone else. It is your responsibility to stay in control of the situation, especially if you are ministering alone. You may have to stand by the person's side in case you need to catch him or her. Always stay alert to what is going on and protect the person from injury.

Occasionally, someone you are praying for may manifest a demon. When I prayed for one woman, the demons in her were stirred up and she began to lose control. If that happens, don't repeat, "Jesus, Jesus, Jesus," even though it's by the name of Jesus that we drive them out. Talk to the person. I had to get this woman's attention back so she could communicate and cooperate in her deliverance.

I asked her name, but she still wasn't in control. So I said, "Do you have any children?"

"Yes."

"How many children do you have?"

Her eyes were still rolling back. We kept up a casual conversation that had nothing to do with standard deliverance practices. I had her repeat her first name, maiden name, and married name until I got her attention back and could converse with **her**. When she was in control of her body and mind, she could pray in agreement to get rid of the demons. After that, she was a totally different person.

3. Listen.

Listen carefully to what the person says and how he or she says it. For example, a car accident always causes trauma. Surgery always creates scar tissue. Pray for discernment from the Holy Spirit as you listen to someone's words. If something is not clear, ask questions.

A team member approached a man who said, "I need you to pray for my hearing."

Putting hands on the man's ears, he prayed, "Father, in the name of Jesus, I curse this deafness. I command it to be gone. I command his hearing to be completely restored and these ears to be open, in Jesus' name. Thank You, Jesus."

Then he asked, "How's your hearing?"

The man answered, "I don't know, my hearing is not until Wednesday."

Many English words have double meanings. Make sure you know what the person is talking about *before* you pray.

4. Touch.

As you pray, whether for yourself or someone else, place one hand on the area that needs healing. If you are praying for someone with a deviated septum or diverticulitis, where do you put your hand? If you don't know, tell the other person, "Put your hand where it hurts." Then no one is embarrassed. The same principle applies to areas of the person's body that are not appropriate for you to lay hands on, especially if the person is a member of the opposite sex. Ask the person to lay hands on the general area and then you lay a hand on his or her hand.

5. Relax.

Relax, and wait on the Lord. There is no need to be nervous or anxious. After you pray, if the person doesn't get healed, listen to what God has to say. He may give you a word of knowledge about a deeper issue, or He may tell you to pray again.

6. Don't give up.

If you pray for someone's needs and the person doesn't get healed, pray against the spirit of trauma. Ask God to show you the root. Then continue your prayer based on what He shows you. Press in and don't give up.

7. Command a new part.

If someone has stomach cancer, first curse the cancer and then pray, "I speak a new stomach, in Jesus' name, and I command the body to be completely restored from any damage because of chemo, radiation, surgery, or medicine. I command complete restoration, in Jesus' name."

If someone has a thyroid problem, how do you pray? Remember, healing is logical: "In the name of Jesus, I speak a new thyroid."

If the problem is diabetes, curse the diabetes, command it to be gone, and then speak a new pancreas.

For a battered or troubled soul, place your hand over the person's heart, curse the trauma, and speak the healing of the emotions and memories. Ask the Lord to show you if the person needs to forgive someone, to confess bitterness or anger, or to be set free from grief or guilt. Carefully phrased, sensitive questions will also help reveal any deeper issues that need prayer. Finally, pray that the person will be filled with joy, peace, hope, and the love of God.

8. Give thanks.

"In everything give thanks; for this is the will of God in Christ Jesus for you" (1 Thessalonians 5:18).

Always, have the person say, "Thank You Jesus."

9. Give God the glory.

Make sure that God gets the glory and not you. If the person focuses more on thanking you than on thanking Jesus, say, "We just watched God answer your prayers."

...And when I heard and saw, I fell down to worship before the feet of the angel who showed me these things. Then he said to me, "See that you do not do that. For I am your fellow servant, and of your brethren the prophets, and of those who keep the words of this book. Worship God" (Revelation 22:8-9).

Jesus always gave His Father the glory. He acknowledged that only by allowing His Father to work through Him was anyone touched or healed by supernatural power. Jesus did His Father's will so the Father would be glorified.

*Do you not believe that I am in the Father, and the Father in Me? The words that I **speak** to you I do not speak on My own authority; but the Father who dwells in Me does the **works**. Believe Me that I am in the Father and the Father in Me, or else believe Me for the sake of the **works** themselves. Most assuredly, I say to you, he who believes in Me, the works that I do he will do also; and greater works than these he will do, because I go to My Father. And whatever*

you ask in My name, that I will do, that the Father may be glorified in the Son. If you ask anything in My name, I will do it (John 14:10-14).

Only through Jesus' total obedience to God throughout His earthly life was God able to bring forth His perfect plan for His children and the world. Have you ever considered what this world would be like if Jesus had said, "NO" at Calvary? He was obedient, He spoke His Father's words, and He did what He saw His Father do. God's perfect plan was put in place for you and for me. God worked everything out for good. Jesus gave God the glory to His last breath.

You must do the same. Never let anyone applaud you. You haven't done anything but follow Jesus' instructions. Have you ever noticed, the Holy Spirit always points to the Son and the Son always defers to the Father? So, who should get the praise and worship? Our Heavenly Father!

How to Pray for Children

Children tend to be timid or shy. They will feel more at ease with a parent present. Get down to their eye level so an unfamiliar adult towering over them does not intimidate them. Keep your tone of voice soft, gentle, and loving. Chat with them for a few minutes and ask a few personal questions to help them relax. Ask them how they feel and ask permission to pray for them. Instruct them to place their hand where it hurts. Do not raise your voice when you pray. Use words that the child can understand. For example, say "tummy" rather than stomach.

Often, praying for the parents first will make the child more receptive to ministry. Be sensitive to the Lord's voice. Sometimes there is a direct connection between the child's condition and a parental need. There might be guilt for the child's illness, stress, or a traumatic event in the home that helped bring on the sickness.

If you suspect that a child has been abused or neglected, it is your legal responsibility to report it to the appropriate authorities, either the local police or the state child protective agency in the county or state where the child resides. You can definitely pray over the situation and people involved; however, the person's safety is paramount. Unfortunately, spousal, parental, or elder abuse also occurs. There are protective services for adults as well as children in every state of the USA. Reporting can be anonymous.

Proxy Prayer Requests

Requests for proxy prayers are an opportunity to encourage people to pray for the healing of their friends, family, others, or themselves. Turn these requests into commissioning prayers. Pray for the person's hands. If possible, instruct them to place one hand on their own heart and the other on the heart of the recipient when they pray.

What to Avoid in Ministering Healing

As important as learning to pray for healing is, it is just as important to learn what to avoid. The following examples help illustrate what *not* to do. Even though I have alluded to some of these things in earlier chapters, I want to remind you again.

If Jesus were on earth today, He would go shopping just like everybody else to buy shoes, clothes, or food. Just as Jesus took the healing power of God with Him to the marketplaces and fishing boats of His day, we are to take His healing power with us wherever we go.

There are some things Jesus would never do. For example, He would never say, "I wish I could pray for that person," or "I just don't feel the anointing right now." Jesus knew He always walked in the anointing. He said, *"The Spirit of the Lord is upon Me, because He has anointed Me"* (Luke 4:18a). As you abide in Him, *"...the anointing which you have received from Him abides in you"* (1 John 2:27a).

Do not wait to "feel" the anointing before you pray for healing for yourself or others. Step out and do it. When you first pray for the sick, your heart may start pounding. That reaction may be from the anointing; however, it could be caused by your own nervousness or fear. Some people report feelings of extreme anticipation or tingling in their hands or heart. As you mature, "feelings" may not happen at all—and you shouldn't expect or depend on them. Like getting married, the "wow" factor might not be there a year or two after the wedding, but the love is still there. Healing can be that way. You don't need to experience the "wow" feeling in order to minister. You know that God's love for people is in you and working through you.

You don't need to drum up the anointing either. Here's another scenario.

"May I pray for you?"

"Yes."

"Don't go anywhere; I'll be right back, OK? Stay right here, OK?" You go to a corner, rubbing your hands together and speaking in tongues in an effort to "feel" the anointing. By the time you muster up the anointing, the person needing prayer has disappeared. Not only that, he or she could report to security: "There's someone over there rubbing his hands together and babbling in a foreign language. Maybe he is dangerous."

You walk by a man who obviously needs healing because he has a cane, crutches, neck brace, and carpal tunnel bands, or is in a wheelchair. Don't tell the man he needs to wait until next month to receive prayer at my meeting. He needs healing now. You are the one God sent. Pray for him.

As you walk by a person, you pray silently, "Father, bless that person." Or you may work up the courage to ask if you can pray for the person but, at the last minute, you veer away, wondering, "What if she doesn't get healed?" Even asking that question means you are taking on the responsibility for the person's healing.

Would Jesus think that way? Who do you think planted that thought? No, it is not the devil; it is your own flesh. The devil does not need to convince you that you can't do it because you've already convinced yourself.

Remember: It's your responsibility to pray and God's responsibility to do the healing. Throw the pressure of false responsibility off yourself, and you will be released to pray for others more often. God is the Creator, not you. He can put a new heart in a person. All you can do is pray, watch, and rejoice once He finishes His work.

You are God's representative. Paul calls you *"ambassadors for Christ"* (2 Cor. 5:20). So leave the healing, or the deliverance, or any other miracle up to God. Once you understand He works miracles through you, then you can say with confidence, *"I can do all things through Christ who strengthens me"* (Phil. 4:13).

Healing comes by His anointing and power flowing through you. Walk in understanding and faith in this foundational truth of His Word and people will be healed when you pray for them.

No "Ifs"

Can you imagine Jesus saying, "Father, if it be Your will, heal them"? God wants everyone healed and walking in divine health. *"...He cast out the spirits with a word, and healed all who were sick"* (Matt. 8:16). As you bury this truth deep within your heart, you will be empowered to flow in the healing ministry with greater faith.

After I prayed, a person said, "The pain didn't go away." I have no control over whether someone is healed or not. I just pray and do what I'm called to do and 90 to 95 percent of the people I pray for do get healed. If someone you pray for isn't healed right away, wait on God and don't give up, but be sure to ask the Holy Spirit what to do.

As I discussed earlier, there may be an underlying cause, such as trauma or a familial curse, which must be handled before the healing manifests. Be open to other alternatives. If the emotional issue is healed, the physical symptoms may disappear without even laying hands on the person.

Progressive Healings

God heals some diseases instantly and others progressively. The timing is always up to Him. As you wait on Him for the full manifestation of your healing, walk out your healing with faith, patience, and perseverance. The healing of some diseases, such as multiple sclerosis, deafness, autism, and Down syndrome sometimes happens over time.

You may pray for someone who is not completely healed. If you discern that the person is healed but needs to wait on the Lord, encourage that person to walk in and maintain the healing with positive faith, even if it takes time.

There is an unusual story in Mark 8:22-25. The blind man wasn't completely healed the first time Jesus laid hands on Him and prayed. Why did Jesus, the Son of God, need to lay hands on him and pray twice? No one knows the answer to that question, but if it happened to Jesus, it can also happen to you.

There is a lesson in this story. If you are not healed the first time you receive prayer, or someone is not totally healed the first time you pray for him or her, do not give up or lose faith. Wait expectantly on Jesus and He will be faithful to complete the work He began.

Then He came to Bethsaida; and they brought a blind man to Him, and begged Him to touch him. So He took the blind man by the hand and led him out of the town. And when He had spit on his eyes and put His hands on him, He asked him if he saw anything. And he looked up and said, "I see men like trees, walking." Then He put His hands on his eyes again and made him look up. And he was restored and saw everyone clearly (Mark 8:22-25).

Through the years, I have received countless testimonies by mail, email, and in person. The stories vary greatly, but they always express God's faithfulness for total healing. Some report they were healed immediately, some over an hour, a day, a week, or a month. Total healing of some situations, such as relationships or marriages, does take a period of time. God is always faithful and keeps His promises.

Healing Without Boundaries

Jesus does not operate within space, time, or other physical limitations. I have ministered by cell phone and email, and people were healed and received new body parts. Nothing limits you but you. Paul wrote to Timothy, *"...I call to remembrance the genuine faith that is in you.... Therefore I remind you to stir up the gift of God which is in you...*" (2 Tim. 1:5-6). Your faith in Him will break through the limits of your expectation of what He can accomplish through you.

However, there are some things that you cannot do, like break generational curses off someone who is not present.

A woman once asked me to pray deliverance over her husband, who had stayed home. If the person is not present and does not want to be set free, deliverance won't happen. I am not limiting the power of God, but if a person's heart is closed, prayer will not free them. God has chosen not to violate our free will. Matthew wrote of Jesus' ministry in Galilee, *"Now He did not do many mighty works there because of their unbelief"* (Matt. 13:58). However, we can pray Ephesians 1:17-19 over such people, that the eyes of their understanding would be enlightened to all that God has for them. This prepares them to listen to, hear, and eventually accept deliverance.

Don't Let Fear Limit You

Don't tell yourself, "If only I had prayed and read my Bible this morning, I could pray for somebody."

Praying for healing is not conditional on how you feel at that moment. If someone with a need walks up to you in the supermarket, don't hesitate. Forgetting to comb your hair or do your makeup does not affect the anointing. Maybe you ran out the door without your quiet time with God. That doesn't affect the anointing either. Maybe it was God urging you to arrive at the supermarket at the perfect time to meet that person in need. You have to put aside concern over your appearance and depend totally on Him. He is present whether you spent time with Him that morning or not.

Your fear reveals who you think is responsible for healing the sick person. Remember, you never rely on yourself—you always rely on Him. Relax when you minister, and don't be afraid that the wrong words might come out of your mouth. He will give you the right words to say. If you speak in tongues, He may give you words in the language only the person you are ministering to understands.

I invited a Christian leader to help pray at an altar call. He came very reluctantly. When suddenly 150 people came up for prayer, he was overwhelmed. He later told the story. A woman approached him while he was trying to remember, "What did Joan say to do?" He reached down, grabbed the woman's wrist and said, "In the name of Jesus, I command these 'tarpal cunnels' to open up." Obviously, he meant carpal tunnel syndrome.

He suddenly realized he hadn't asked her what she needed. He apologized. She said, "My hands were numb and now they're not." God knew what she needed. The man heard God and acted. God makes up the difference even if you make a mistake.

Remember, you don't have to be in perfect health to pray for others. The Word says, "*...pray for one another, that you may be healed. The effective, fervent prayer of a righteous man avails much*" (James 5:16). Get out of your comfort zone and don't be embarrassed or self-conscious. Just start doing what Jesus did and diseases will fall off you, also.

Don't Limit God

Never limit God as to how or what He can and will accomplish. "*...with God all things are possible*" (Mark 10:27).

Walking in the miraculous requires faith that is "*...sure of what we hope for and certain of what we do not see*" (Heb. 11:1 NIV). Thomas did not believe the other disciples when they told him they had seen the risen Lord, even though Jesus Himself had predicted His resurrection. Jesus exhorted Thomas not to limit God with an "I have to see it to believe it" attitude:

Now Thomas, called the Twin, one of the twelve, was not with them when Jesus came. The other disciples therefore said to him, "We have seen the Lord." So he said to them, "Unless I see in His hands the print of the nails, and put my finger into the print of the nails, and put my hand into His side, I will not believe."

And after eight days His disciples were again inside, and Thomas with them. Jesus came, the doors being shut, and stood in the midst, and said, "Peace to you!" Then He said to Thomas, "Reach your finger here, and look at My hands; and reach your hand here, and put it into My side. Do not be unbelieving, but believing." And Thomas answered and said to Him, "My Lord and my God!" Jesus said to him, "Thomas, because you have seen Me, you have believed. Blessed are those who have not seen and yet have believed" (John 20:24-29).

God is the Creator. He can create anything you need. God is the Healer. He can heal any illness you can have. Everything belongs to Him. He can direct finances and people into your life to bless you at any moment. He wrote the manual to guide you and will open your eyes to His truth. He is truth, so you can count on every promise in His Word.

Jesus is the same yesterday, today, and forever. He healed in the Old Testament. He healed in the New Testament. He heals today, and He will heal tomorrow forever.

Don't ever limit God and what He wants to do through you. He can and will do whatever He wants to do with a willing, believing, obedient child.

Jesus Is Our Healer

Know in your heart, mind, and spirit that God wants to use you. You have to be willing and available. When you see someone sick, something will happen to you on the inside.

Just as the Jesus living in you wants to reach out and touch them, your healing hands and heart will reach out to that person, also. Everyone is within three feet of a miracle—the length of your outstretched arms. The power of God using the Holy Ghost laser heals in Jesus' name. You are just the conduit. Learn, go, and do likewise.

CHAPTER ELEVEN

RECEIVE AND MAINTAIN YOUR HEALING

Many people have received healing and appear to have lost it. Is it God's fault? NO! Does God take away His blessings? NO. What happened? Were they faking their healing? Why wasn't the person healed?

While some people put up obstacles to pray for healing, others consciously or unconsciously hinder their own healing. Recognize these hindrances, both in your own life and in the lives of those you pray for. I can't say this enough, God is the healer, not you. Healing is in His hands, not yours. It is His responsibility to heal, not yours. He knows the details of every person's life. You don't.

I want to share some positive things you can do to fully possess and maintain divine health. You may also be teaching others during your ministry.

Let Go

Don't let sickness become your friend. What do I mean by that? Some people enjoy the pity and extra attention they get when they are sick. Friends, family, church members, and others may cook and clean for them or do special favors while they are ill. Before they know it, the pity and attention they receive from others becomes an emotional crutch. This can become a subtle hindrance to walking in divine health.

If healing occurs, you may have to give up the "Disabled Person" license plate or tag hanging in your car that gives you special parking privileges. Perhaps you will have to give up your government disability income or food stamps because you no longer qualify. You can now be gainfully employed! Your vision is restored so you can go to school and study!

Some people don't want to give up their disability and the attention they receive. Sounds strange, but they enjoy being sick. Their identity has become wrapped up in their disability. They are afraid of losing their way of life if they are healed. They hang onto it for dear life even though they claim to want healing.

When Peter and John prayed for a lame man at the temple in Jerusalem, they didn't pray at first for the man's physical healing (see Acts 3:1-7). Peter first addressed the lame man's expectation— the only thing he asked for was alms (see Acts 3:3).

And fixing his eyes on him, with John, Peter said, "Look at us." So he gave them his attention, expecting to receive something from them (see Acts 3:4-5).

What are you expecting to receive from those around you? All the lame man was expecting was a few coins. After Peter made sure he had the man's attention:

Then Peter said, "Silver and gold I do not have, but what I do have I give you: In the name of Jesus Christ of Nazareth, rise up and walk." And he took him by the right hand and lifted him up, and immediately his feet and ankle bones received strength. So he, leaping up, stood and walked and entered the temple with them—walking, leaping, and praising God (Acts 3:6-8).

Do you want to be healed? Put emotional or spiritual lameness and the "alms" of pity and attention behind you and receive the healing power of Jesus. He will set you free and lead you into a new walk with God.

Denial

Sometimes you don't handle a sickness or challenging situation in the right way. Instead of dealing with it, you cram it down inside. It festers inside you and turns into bitterness. Has this happened to you?

People ask, "How are you?"

You answer, "I'm fine," when you are not fine at all?

Yes, positive affirmation and the power in words are both very important. However, there is a time and place to ask for help. When a man or woman of God asks if you need something, respond. God is speaking through that person and wants to help you.

Putting on a façade of perfection doesn't help you or the people around you. Everyone has his or her challenges. What you do with those challenges is the key. If you hurt, do you moan, groan, and complain? Or do you go directly to God? Maybe God wants you to share your situation with others. They need to pray for you as much as you need to pray for them. Set the example. Admit you aren't perfect. Don't be afraid to admit you have needs also.

Teamwork

As a Christian, you belong to a family of believers who help each other. When one part of the body hurts, the rest of the body hurts. Share your needs, pray in agreement, and share your miracles, whether big or small. God cares about the everyday issues of life as well as the big things. Practice working together. When the victory comes, everyone can rejoice together.

Hiding a problem behind the comment, "I'm fine!" is a habit. It is not walking in truth. If you are "fine", you are saying, "I don't need anything. I don't need prayer." Jesus said in Mark 2:17, *"Those who are well have no need of a physician."* Draw close to Jesus and confess every need to Him. He desires you to be healed and whole, full of the Holy Spirit, and set free to operate in the gifts of the Spirit—including the healing of others.

When Dad ministered the baptism of the Holy Spirit, he would sometimes choose one of the newly committed Christians and guide the new believer through healing another person. Imagine, a brand-new Christian ministering healing to someone else! The eight-year-old daughter of a friend was chosen at one of the Minnesota meetings. She had to stand on a chair to reach the forehead of a six-foot man who needed healing. She obeyed the man of God, prayed, and watched in amazement as this giant of a man fell out under the power of the Holy Spirit and rose up healed. Thirty some years later, she still remembers and reaches out to heal others.

Setting yourself up as perfect can often negatively impact other Christians. They may get the impression that only the perfect can pray for another. Encourage and mentor others to pray for each other and to pray for you as well.

Am I always 100 percent well? No! I am human and I have health challenges. The enemy doesn't stop trying to keep me from my calling. However, I have a team of armor bearers around the world who keep me in prayer 24/7. When I have a need, I ask for prayer. Teamwork.

You want to receive and keep your healing? Develop a team to build each other up with prayer and the Word of God whether in person, by letter, on the Web, or by phone.

You are not too young or too old. You are not too small or too big. You have not done something in your past that was so bad that God can't forgive. If He could use David (a murderer and adulterer), He can use you. If He could use Paul (a murderer of Christians) to evangelize most of the known world in his day, He can use you. If He could use Rahab (a prostitute), He can use you.

Stop making excuses. He has heard them all, forgiven you, and still loves you.

Witness

Who gets the glory if you deny your healing? Who gets the glory if you broadcast your healing? Whose faith is built up if you share your testimony with others?

Yes, you are to witness to others about your salvation and the Gospel of Jesus Christ. However, have you ever considered the witness you are when you have been healed?

Years ago, a person walked up to a family who were going through some very serious spiritual battles. Newly committed to Christ, they were feeling totally overwhelmed by the enemy's attacks. This wise, mature Christian looked the mother in the eye and said, "You have no idea how many people are watching you and your family. Will you hang onto God or will you fall back to the world for answers to your problems? We are praying for you."

What a powerful revelation! Do you have any idea how many people you are touching just by being a walking witness? Your healing is a witness. Your attitude toward ministering to others is a witness. Being willing to pray for someone is a witness. Will you welcome a coworker who needs help during your lunch break? Can someone call you in the middle of the night for prayer? Are you willing to give up some sleep to obey God's whispered orders to pray?

Be a walking witness for Christ.

Rebuke the Lies

The enemy does not want you well. He does not want you healthy, happy, and ministering God's love and healing power to your neighbors, your city, your state, or around the world. He will try anything to stop you. His weapons include lies, deceit, hate, anger, frustration, as well as all the other negative feelings and actions in his arsenal.

But you have Jesus, the personification of God's love living within you. Remember Jesus' arguments in the desert with satan when He was tempted and tested by His #1 enemy. He answered every time with the Word of God.

Don't listen to the "woe is me" comments of the world. Listen to the positive words of your Father. Find His promises in His Word. Memorize them. Repeat them to yourself often. Post His Word around your home if necessary. Play praise and worship songs in your home and car. Let your soul and spirit absorb His words and love through every pore in your body.

His words are life. Jesus said, *"The Spirit gives life; the flesh counts for nothing. The words I have spoken to you are spirit and they are life"* (John 6:63 NIV). (See also Psalm 119:50.)

The world will drag you down into the pit of hell. His Word will take you to Heaven. It is your choice. Surround yourself with people filled with Him who will encourage you, pray for you, and keep you focused. You may have to find new friends. You may also have to change the way you speak. Speaking positive words will keep your glass half-full. Looking for the good in situations and people will keep you appreciative and praising God.

By staying positive and focused on His promises, you are actively rebuking the enemy and his lies. Read God's Word daily, even if it is just one or two verses. Do something for Him every day. Soon you will be doing more and more for Him. You will become spiritually healthy as well as physically healthy.

A friend told me a story about my dad from years ago. During a meeting, Dad was speaking. Every 5-10 minutes, he would say, "Excuse me," and disappear behind the podium. He would pop back up after 5-10 seconds and continue on ministering. He did this several times during the meeting. No one in the audience knew what was going on. It didn't seem to fit into the meeting or his message. Later, it was revealed that Dad was feeling the effects of the "flu" that was going around. When he felt the urge to vomit, he excused himself and reached for the bucket that was available behind the podium. He didn't allow the enemy to stop the message or what God wanted to accomplish through him that day.

Don't accept the lies the enemy throws at you! "You aren't healed!" "No one will get healed through you!" "Once sick, always sick!" "God can't really fix your back!" "Why get your hopes up?"

You will hear those words. You may hear them time and time again. However, you neither accept them nor repeat them! You find His Words and His promises! You find someone to agree with you in prayer! You concentrate on Him and His will for your life!

CHAPTER TWELVE

YOUR TOOLBOX

They will lay hands on the sick, and they will recover (Mark 16:18b).

Thank You, Jesus, for allowing me to fulfill the calling on my life. Thank You for allowing me to lay hands on the sick and to see them recover, according to the Word of God.

His Gift, Your Tools

Your desire to grow in the use of God's gifts has brought you to this place in your journey with Him. Your study of this healing manual will open the door to increased wisdom and knowledge that will empower you to heal the sick and make the brokenhearted whole in spirit, mind, body, soul, and finances.

In this manual, you will find revelation based on His Word. Yes, you can read and learn from this manual, but you can always go to the Master's Manual, God's Word, and get further revelation and details. What Jesus did, you can do. His Word says so. Research it for yourself. He gives you what you need to fulfill His call on your life.

God has a special reward for your faithfulness—a personal toolbox created specifically for you and the mission before you. In your toolbox, you will find:

- Powerful words to pray that pinpoint the root of sickness and disease like a laser.

- Revelation and words of knowledge for the person you are praying for that only God can reveal to you. (Later you may not remember anything you said.)

- Dreams and visions that will lead, guide, and direct your pathway with specific instructions.

- Keys to unlock the hidden and powerful mysteries of God.

- Supernatural gifts of wisdom and discernment.

- Divine appointments and connections.

- Miracles, signs, and wonders as God moves through you.

We stand together in agreement as you pray and ask God for your personal toolbox.

In an attitude of worship and reverence toward God, hold out your arms in front of you with your hands open and palms up, and pray this prayer:

Father God, I surrender to You and I commit these hands to You for Your glory and work for the rest of my days. I stand before You ready to receive my toolbox filled with supernatural tools that only You can impart, so I can go forth to heal the sick and perform signs, wonders, and miracles. Amen. Thank You, Jesus!

Your acceptance of your toolbox has a price and an expectation. It requires spending time with the Lord and for your ears and heart to remain open to His guidance to use and develop your gifts.[1]

Congratulations as you embark on your calling and place in God's healing army, birthed by the Holy Spirit out of a remnant of believers.[2]

HAVE YOU CONSIDERED:

1. Are you a walking witness?_____
   _____
   _____

2. Do your closest friends know you will pray for them anytime and anywhere they ask?_____
   _____
   _____

3. Are you ready to be a new wineskin for His anointing?
   _____
   _____
   _____

4. Have you felt His anointing? _____
   _____
   _____
   _____

5. If He asks, what are you willing to give up for Him?
   _____
   _____
   _____
   _____

ENDNOTES

1. 4 Corners Alliance: A body of believers united together to complement the call and vision for your ministry under the apostolic healing covering of Joan Hunter.

2. JHM: Joan Hunter Ministries equips and activates believers to fulfill Mark 16:18.

Prayers For Freedom

Doing It His Way, Use the Gifts He Has Given You

This manual is a handbook for successful Kingdom ministry. All effective ministry must be led by God. The Word of God and the Holy Spirit working together through His Body heal the sick and save the lost. All power belongs to God and all effective ministry flows through Him alone.

Read His Word. Listen to His voice. Believe His truth. Obey His instructions. Praise Him for always keeping His promises. Jesus told His followers that they would do greater things than He had done (see John 14:12). Since He is the same yesterday, today, and tomorrow (see Heb. 13:8), that means all His followers will be doing the same. You and I are those followers and will do greater miracles than He did during His lifetime if we obey the Word and follow the Holy Spirit.

Jesus did and said what His Father did and said. With Jesus living in you, you should do likewise. Reach out as He guides you. Speak the words He gives you. Heal the sick. Restore lives. Give Him the praise and the glory for every miracle you see or hear about.

The following prayers are not flowery or complex. They are very simple. Do they work? Every prayer has successfully brought healing, restoration, and reconciliation to countless thousands around the world.

This manual does not contain a prayer for every physical ailment or injury you may encounter. It does have some of the most common prayers I use. Use them until they become second nature to you and soon they will flow out of you without effort or thought as you minister God's healing power to others.

Jesus did not use theatrics. He did not yell, spit, or push people over. He simply spoke truth into the situation at hand.

People can be healed with a whisper. However, the sick person does need to think, say, and hear the words. Active participation (thinking, saying, and hearing) often stops negative thoughts from derailing the healing process. The enemy will do anything to interrupt any form of restoration. Repeating the positive scriptural examples will embed those words firmly into the memory and increase their effectiveness.

GENERAL PRAYER

Often people or, specifically, children cannot verbalize the specific disease or problem they are experiencing. They describe their condition as: "I just don't feel good. I don't know what to ask for. I just need help."

Ask God to show you what to pray. However, if you don't receive any specific words of knowledge, use this prayer as it applies:

Father, in the name of Jesus, I curse the spirit of trauma and fear and command it to go. I speak life to the immune system and health to the bones. I command the bad to go and energy to be restored. Thank You, Jesus.

HEART AND CIRCULATION ISSUES
THE CARDIOVASCULAR SYSTEM

My flesh and my heart fail; but God is the strength of my heart and my portion forever (Psalm 73:26).

When you pray for someone with a heart problem, ask for the doctor's diagnosis so you can pray specifically for the exact illness. Like other diseases, heart problems can be a result of stress, trauma, poor diet, lack of exercise, generational curses, or other factors. One methodology does not fit every situation, so ask enough questions to understand the person's needs.

Prayer for the Heart Plus...

A woman came for prayer. She explained her heart had a leaky valve and she had some difficulties from a car accident. She was unable to sleep while lying on one side of her head because of pain and only warmth eased the pain.

Praying for trauma and nothing else would take care of her head. Since she was diagnosed with a heart problem, she needed prayer for her heart as well. A leaky heart valve can cause fatigue and minor memory loss due to a lack of oxygen reaching the brain.

Father, in the name of Jesus, I curse the spirit of trauma and fear. I command it to be gone, in Jesus' name. I command all pain to leave this head and for this neck to go into perfect alignment and for the head to go back on the proper axis, in Jesus' name.

I command the pH balance and all electromagnetic frequencies in this body to come into perfect balance and harmony, in Jesus' name. I speak a new, healthy heart with no leaky valves or any other problem. I speak total restoration of the circulation in the heart as well as the rest of the body. Thank You, Jesus.

Generational Curses

All generational curses are first broken by repentence. Then we ask God to remove the symptoms.

Father, forgive me and my ancestors for our sins. Put them on the cross, never to be held against me again in Jesus' name. Thank You, Jesus.

High Blood Pressure

Father, in the name of Jesus, I break the generational curse of high blood pressure that has come through the family blood-line. I command health and wholeness for this vascular system and for the systolic and diastolic pressure to normalize. I curse any plaque buildup in the arteries and I speak the opening, elasticity, and proper functioning of all blood vessels, in Jesus' name. I command the blood pressure to return to normal.

Have the person you are praying for repeat this after you:

Father, forgive me for carrying burdens that belong to You and stress on my own shoulders. I lay them all on Your altar, in Jesus' name. Give me wisdom in my diet, exercise, and lifestyle. Thank You, Jesus.

High Cholesterol

Father, in the name of Jesus, I break any generational curses of high cholesterol and I command all cholesterol levels in this body to return to normal. I speak healing and continued health to all arteries affected by plaque buildup, and I curse that plaque and command it to dissolve into the bloodstream and pass out of the body, in Jesus' name. I command a healthy, properly functioning vascular system, in Jesus' name. Thank You, Jesus.

If necessary, ask the person you are praying for to repeat: *Father, forgive me for not following the proper diet.*

Because someone with a heart problem may also be dealing with the fear of dying, dealing with that fear is also very important.

Father, in Jesus' name, I curse the spirit of death and fear off this body. I command it to go. Thank You, Jesus.

Lung and Breathing Problems

Sore Throat

Viruses are the most common cause of sore throats, and they often lead to upper respiratory infections. However, a sore throat can also be the result of acid reflux; allergies; dry, frigid air; muscle strain—like shouting too much at a football game—exposure to pollutants such as smoke; a bacterial infection, such as strep throat; or other factors.

Before you pray for someone who is complaining of throat pain, ask questions so that your prayers can be focused because there may be underlying factors.

Father, in the name of Jesus, I command all that pain and inflammation to go. I curse the virus and I command it to be gone, in Jesus' name. Thank You, Jesus.

A woman I will call Cece came forward who was obviously having problems with laryngitis. She thought it was caused by a virus and could vocalize only a few sounds. During the interview, she shared that her husband had recently had surgery. After coming home, he started to hemorrhage and had to return to the hospital.

The trauma of her husband's illness affected her voice. I prayed:

I command that bleeding to stop with no more complications, in Jesus' name. I curse this spirit of trauma and I command it to go. I speak health and wholeness to the throat and larynx, in Jesus' name. I curse this laryngitis and any pain or inflammation associated with it, and I command it to go, in Jesus' name. Thank You, Jesus.

Cece's next words were clear and spoken without pain!

Chronic Respiratory Diseases

Allergies can cause inflammation of the mucous membranes in the nose, throat, and eyes, causing reddened eyes, runny nose, and headaches. Asthma, emphysema, and chronic bronchitis can be caused by numerous irritating factors in the environment. All of these respiratory diseases can be very uncomfortable and often debilitating as they affect more and more delicate pulmonary tissue. Smoking is often a factor whether a person is currently using tobacco or if he or she stopped years ago. Tobacco's effects are permanent.

Place your hand on the person's upper chest near the throat and pray:

Father, in Jesus' name, I curse the spirit of trauma and fear on this person and I command it to leave. I speak two new lungs free from asthma, emphysema, and bronchitis, and I command this body to stop overreacting to environmental irritants. Thank You, Jesus.

Gastrointestinal and Digestion Difficulties

Choking

A man described a continuous sore throat. He could swallow, but he felt like he was choking sometimes. "I think it's my esophagus. Food doesn't go down easily."

Father, in the name of Jesus, I curse the spirit of trauma and fear. I command all choking to stop and all the throat muscles to relax, in Jesus' name. I speak health and wholeness throughout this entire digestive system, and I command all pain and inflammation of the throat to go, in Jesus' name. Thank You, Jesus.

Several years earlier, something had lodged in his throat. The trauma was still there. It was gone after prayer. Swallowing became natural again.

Indigestion, Ulcers, Irritable Bowel Syndrome, Constipation

There are numerous diseases that can affect the digestive tract from eating to elimination of waste, such as eating disorders, irritations, bleeding, tumors, diverticulitis, hernias, constipation, diarrhea, indigestion, reflux...the list goes on.

Father, in the name of Jesus, I curse the spirit of trauma and fear. I curse any spirit of control to be gone. I command the hernia to disappear, the muscles to close up, and increased strength to the abdominal muscles. I command all constipation to stop and all the gastrointestinal muscles to relax, in Jesus' name. I speak health and wholeness throughout this entire digestive system, and I command all pain and inflammation to go. I command all stress and residual effects of stress to be gone, in Jesus' name. Thank You, Jesus.

ENDOCRINE SYSTEMS: DIABETES AND THYROID

The abnormal blood sugar levels caused by diabetes will also damage the nerves, kidneys, circulation, vision, and heart of the individual. So just praying healing for the pancreas is not enough. You must pray for complete restoration of the other organs of the body that have also been damaged. Frequently, diabetics will end up with neuropathy (numbness of the hands or feet), kidney failure, gangrene leading to amputations of the toes or feet (circulation), blindness, or silent heart attacks. That list doesn't include the episodes of very high or low blood sugars that can cause comas, unconsciousness, or death.

Prayer should be focused on a new endocrine system and a new pancreas. Then you should go on with restoration to the rest of the body to prevent any other issues from developing later.

Enlargement, goiters, or nonfunctioning thyroids can occur in both men and women. The hormones produced by this tiny organ near the vocal cords affects energy levels and the body's metabolic rate. Too little thyroid hormone production causes sluggishness, weakness, cold intolerance, and excessive weight gain. Too much causes hyperactivity, weight loss, nervousness, and palpitations. This hormone affects many other bodily functions also.

You can pray for the heart, as an example, because of the palpitations. The problem could be caused by thyroid issues, not heart disease.

Father, in Jesus' name, I curse the spirit of trauma and the effects of trauma on this body, especially the entire endocrine system.

For diabetes, add: *I curse diabetes and speak a new pancreas that is fully functional, producing insulin in the proper amount. I command the sugar level to return to the normal range.*

For thyroid, add: *I speak a new thyroid into this body. I command the energy level to return to normal. I command the goiter to be gone. Thank You, Jesus.*

Reproduction Abnormalities: Reproductive System and Hormones

Since problems with menstruation, hormones, sexual function, and reproductive organs are common, there will always be people needing prayer for these issues.

Menstrual Problems

Many menstrual symptoms, such as irregularity, are caused by an imbalance of hormones. Place the woman's hand(s) on her abdominal area or on both hipbones. If a male is praying, the man's hand(s) should be placed over the woman's hand(s). Ministry will include rotation of the pelvis as described in the musculoskeletal portion of this section. Pray:

For Women's pelvic or hormonal problems, another woman should lay hands on both hipbones or over the abdomen.

Father, in the name of Jesus, I command this pelvic area to rotate and go into its proper position. I command all the female organs to go into their proper position and for the restoration of

regular function. I command all hormones to be in perfect harmony and balance, in Jesus' name. Thank You, Jesus.

For women's pelvic or hormonal problems, another woman should lay hands on both hipbones or over the abdomen.

Premenstrual Syndrome

Premenstrual syndrome, commonly known as PMS, is caused by female hormonal imbalance. If you haven't experienced it yourself, you probably know someone who has. Some women affected by this syndrome believe they have a right to verbally abuse others and make them miserable for five days of each month. PMS does not give any woman permission to misuse anyone else. If you have ever gotten verbally abusive at that time of the month and said things you ordinarily wouldn't say, sit down with your spouse when neither of you are having hormonal problems and have an honest, conciliatory conversation. For PMS, pray:

In the name of Jesus, I command the hormones to return to perfect harmony and balance. Thank You, Jesus.

If you have verbally abused anyone, ask God and the person for forgiveness.

Infertility

Infertility can occur in a man or a woman for various reasons. Spiritual hindrances could include the need to sever a generational curse or unholy covenant. Problems with the reproductive organs and processes, or stress-induced imbalance to the body's pH levels—its alkalinity or acidity—can also prevent pregnancy. Lead both the husband and wife in a prayer for these issues. If the couple is not married, they need the benefit of counseling and a prayer of repentance, not a prayer for pregnancy. There are a variety of physical reasons why a husband and wife may not be able to achieve pregnancy. Pray:

Father, Your Word says, "Behold, children are a heritage from the Lord, the fruit of the womb is a reward" (Ps. 127:3). And in accordance with the Word of God, we thank You, in Jesus' name, for Your promise of the fruit of the womb to _____ and _____ . I take authority in the name of Jesus over all hindrances to conception and command both pelvises to come into position and all the reproductive organs to function properly. In Jesus' name. I command the pH levels in these bodies to come into perfect balance. We thank You for a baby within one year! Thank You, Jesus.

Hot Flashes

Some women experience hot flashes during menopause. During this unpleasant but normal change within the female body, estrogen levels drop suddenly. A woman gets dressed up, reaches a destination, turns red, and starts sweating profusely. After awhile, she may complain she is too cold until the next "hot flash" occurs. It is very unpleasant and uncontrollable. When someone has a hormonal swing with these symptoms, immediately pray:

In the name of Jesus, I curse these hot flashes and I command them to be gone. I command the hormones and the electrical and magnetic frequencies in this body to return to perfect harmony and balance, in Jesus' name. Thank You, Jesus.

(This prayer will work whether or not the woman still has ovaries or a uterus. Postmenopausal symptoms occur after surgical removal of female organs also.)

At a meeting with evangelists and authors, I noticed a woman in the front row bobbing up and down. I asked her what she was doing, and she said, "I have hot flashes." With every hot flash she bent down and got a battery powered fan out of her purse to fan herself. When she cooled down, she would put the fan back and sit up again. Her husband was proud of all the batteries he carried in his pocket to power the fan.

After I prayed with her, she did not experience any more "flashes." Now this family is in the healing ministry. Use your batteries for microphones to minister to His people, not on fans for hot flashes!

Male Hormone Problems

Men have hormone level changes, too, although they don't talk about it the way women do. No matter how well men know each other, they are not going to discuss that subject. Only a few are even willing to talk to a doctor who can help to ease their symptoms.

As men get older, they experience a lull in their hormone levels. At that point, men lose their drive—not only their sexual drive, but also their drive and verve for life. They can develop depression or become couch potatoes. Prayer for the restoration of normal hormone levels is not only for enhanced physical health—it is also a prayer for vitality and quality of life.

In the name of Jesus, I curse these symptoms and I command them to be gone. I command the hormones and the electrical and magnetic frequencies in this body to return to perfect harmony and balance, in Jesus' name. Thank You, Jesus.

NEUROLOGICAL AND NERVE IRREGULARITIES

Stroke

A stroke occurs when there is a blockage or interruption of blood to a portion of the brain. Without the oxygen carried in the blood, cells of the brain die, stopping communication to a portion of the body and causing paralysis and loss of function. Loss of memory, inability to speak, paralysis, or weakness of one side of the body are common manifestations after a stroke. If severe, death follows. Occasionally, these symptoms only last a few hours or a few days and are called a "mini" stroke. A warning sign of a larger stroke to come, these small incidents must not be ignored. The blockages are caused by blood clots, a ruptured blood vessel, or small pieces of plaque from arteriosclerosis of other blood vessels in the body.

Father, I curse the death assignment this trauma has brought to this body. I speak a new brain into this body. I command normal function be restored to every cell in this body. I command every nerve, every muscle, and every ligament to function normally, in Jesus' name.

Alzheimer's Disease

A serious debilitating disease affecting an ever increasing number of people, Alzheimer's disease actually affects everyone in the family. Premature or total dementia causes major changes to the family structure and lifestyle. Wandering, disruptive behaviors, personality changes, inability to feed or dress one's self, and total dependence on caregivers are only a part of the challenge to care for loved ones suffering from these changes within the brain.

The cause baffles doctors and scientists. Most relatives are told to adjust to the worst possible scenario and not to expect a return to normalcy. If this happens to you, immediately cut those words off in Jesus' name.

Father, I curse the disease of Alzheimer's and dementia from this body as well as the trauma it has caused in this family. I command every brain cell to function normally with good memory and bodily control. I speak the fluid levels in the brain to return to proper amounts. I speak the electrical and chemical balance be restored along all the nerve pathways, in Jesus' name.

Numbness / Loss of Sensation / Neuropathy

Any disruption of the electrical pathways of the nervous system can cause numbness to a portion of the body. Swelling or edema from an injury, decreased circulation, bones out of place, or abnormal blood levels can be life-threatening. Feeling or sensation tells you things within your body are OK or that something is wrong. For instance, not feeling pain in your foot can hide a blister, an open wound, infection, or interruption of circulation. Your foot can be bleeding with a serious injury. Without your knowledge, you can be in serious trouble, lose a foot, or die. There are some people who feel no pain. It is not a blessing from God.

Father, I curse whatever has caused this loss of sensation. I command feeling be restored in the hands, legs, feet, and/or fingers. I speak normal function to all circulation and nerves that have been affected, in Jesus' name.

MUSCULOSKELETAL, BONE, TENDONS, AND MUSCLE CHANGES

Which of you by worrying can add one cubit to his stature? (Matthew 6:27)

Skeletal and Spinal Disorders

More people request prayer for back problems than for any other physical need. More than 26 million Americans between the ages of 20 to 64 suffer from ongoing back pain, one of the primary reasons for visits to a doctor's office.[1]

When you minister to someone with back or neck pain, you need to understand the basic anatomy of the back and spine. The spinal column and its 31 pairs of spinal nerves is an extension of the brain, and, with it, forms the central nervous system. Muscles and ligaments support the vertebrae and spinal column. With age, bone strength, muscle tone, and flexibility decline, making the possibility of injury or strain—and resulting pain, tingling, or numbness—more likely. When the spinal column is out of alignment, a pinched nerve can cut off the surrounding spinal fluid that cushions it, resulting in pain. When someone you are praying for complains of pain in the C-3, D-11, or L-2, they are referring to one of the cervical (neck), dorsal (or thoracic—portion of the back where ribs are connected), or lumbar (lower back) vertebrae.

The discs of the spinal column act like small cushions between each vertebra—the small bones that form the backbone. These discs keep the vertebrae apart and give flexibility to the spine. If a vertebra is twisted, the disc protrudes at one end and no longer protects the other side of the vertebra. This herniated disc pinches nerves traveling throughout the body, causing pain.

Degenerative disc disease weakens the bones of the spine. Osteoporosis, osteoarthritis, and crushed vertebrae or discs often result in a loss of height. Once healed, people usually regain their original height.

In osteoporosis, the bones weaken, become porous, fragile, and break very easily. Osteopenia is the precursor to osteoporosis. In women, it often begins with menopause. Exercise and a calcium-rich diet help prevent osteopenia and osteoporosis. There are no symptoms in this silent but deadly disease. Falls or even sudden movement can result in fractures, which can leave the person immobilized.

The bones of the body form the structures to protect vital organs and allow a person to stand upright and walk. With osteoporosis, even an innocent cough can cause a fractured rib that can puncture a lung, causing death. The wrong turn of a porous leg bone can become a hip fracture and leave the person wheelchair-bound. A break of a bone in the spine can cause paralysis.

The coccyx, or tailbone, can be broken or bumped out of position, causing pain. Scoliosis, a lateral curvature of the spine, can cause uneven shoulders, hips, or waist alignment. Scoliosis may be caused by heredity or a generational curse, arthritis of the spine, or one leg being shorter than the other.

After you pray for someone with a back injury or condition, differentiate between lingering soreness or stiffness and pain. The pain and what caused it should go, but people may have to work out soreness or stiffness in the muscles or joints that have not been used normally over a long period of time.

The following testimonies and prayers are examples of ministry to several varieties of back and neck problems.

Holy Spirit Spinal Surgery

During one meeting, a man could barely hobble up to the front of the room. Asking for prayer, he explained that none of the vertebrae in his back were working properly.

I told him, "You need a new spine." He looked doubtful. Then suddenly, out of the corner of my eye, I saw something flash by and the man gave a little startle and exclaimed, "I just got a new spine!" I hadn't even prayed yet.

About ten minutes later, another man came up to the platform. All I said was, "You need a new spine." Whoosh. There went another one.

An employee praying over the phone at my office suddenly saw a vision of a spine going through the phone. The woman on the end of the line said, "I just got a new spine!"

Testimony—New Discs

When you pray for someone who has lost height, gently put your hands around his throat. Cup your thumbs very gently underneath his ears with your fingertips pointed toward each other at the back of his neck. This will help you feel the person grow taller.

A woman came forward for prayer. She had lost three inches in height because her discs had collapsed with osteoporosis. As I was preparing to minister to her, she closed her eyes and started to pray.

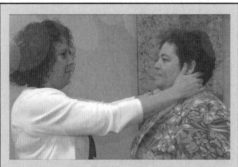

Gently place your hands around a person's neck when you pray for the restoration of vetebrae and discs, or for osteoarthritis. That way you can feel the miracle when the person's height is restored.

If people are talking or even praising God while I am praying, 90 percent don't get healed. If Jesus was talking to you, you wouldn't bow your head and start praying. First of all, it would be rude. With the King of kings in front of you, your eyes would be wide open looking into His beautiful face. Jesus lives in me. I am His representative and I ask people to look at me. Gently tell the person to keep her eyes open, look at you, and pay attention. The person can talk to God and thank Jesus after she is healed.

Father, in the name of Jesus, I curse the spirit of trauma. I command it to be gone and for all pain to go. I speak a healthy new spine, all new vertebrae and discs restored, and full height to be restored, in Jesus' name.

Sometimes you can feel people getting taller. Sometimes they can feel it as real bone returns to their spine, although, total restoration of height may take some time. When the healing is manifested, their sleeves may appear too short or they may be looking down at you instead of up. Don't forget to have them thank Jesus!

Herniated Disc and Neck Pain

While ministering for these problems, I have the people hold their hands out straight in front of them, not touching but fairly close together. One arm is often a little longer than the

other. The symptoms may include neck pain, tingling in the face, as well as pain in other areas of the back. Pray:

Father, in the name of Jesus, I speak new discs into this neck in Jesus' name. I command the ligaments and tendons to function normally and the arms to be even with each other, every bit of pain to go, in Jesus' name. Thank You, Jesus.

Have them check their neck. Sometimes the pain is gone, but the neck may still be a little sore. Ask them to repeat after you:

In the name of Jesus, I speak new discs and a new vertebrae in my back. I command all the pain to go in Jesus' name. Thank You, Jesus.

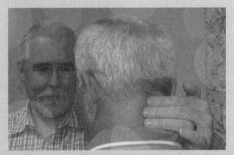

Degenerative disc disease or arthritis of the spine can cause neck pain. Lay hands on the neck and pray against the pain and the disease, or other cause.

Tell the people to check their back. Instruct them to touch their toes. When they stand before you, healed and totally amazed at what God has done for them, tell them to say, "Thank You, Jesus!"

A Back Accident

Through a word of knowledge, God revealed to me that someone in a meeting had experienced a falling accident that jammed his back, causing pain. The person also had lost two or three inches of height. A gentleman acknowledged the exact symptoms I had described. He had had an accident in 1966 in a mine in Australia and suffered with back problems ever since. He had never paid attention to how much height he had lost. As he stood in front of me relating these details, I could tell God was healing him before I even started praying. He was already getting taller. I prayed:

Father, I curse the spirit of trauma, in Jesus' name. I command all that to go. I speak health and wholeness to this spine and I command this body to continue to grow the rest of the way. In the name of Jesus, I command the spine to straighten out, and all pain to go. Thank You, Jesus.

As he said, "Thank You, Jesus!" he was obviously taller and reported the discomfort was gone. Instead of his eyes being below my shoulder level, he could look over my shoulder. God is so amazing!

Back Injury Healed

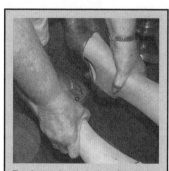

For lower back pain, check the length of both legs. If one is shorter, pray for the leg to grow and the pain to go.

Many people have one leg that is shorter than the other. This abnormal positioning puts pressure on the spine and supporting muscles. When praying for the lower back, ask the person to sit down so you can measure his or her legs. Ask the person to relax his or her legs so you or your prayer partner can hold the feet off the floor. Place your thumbs on the anklebones as you pray and command the shorter leg to grow, in Jesus' name.

A woman was thrown by a horse 30-plus years before and landed on the small of her back. Arthritis set in around the injured bones. She came forward for ministry. I had her sit down as usual and I measured her legs. One leg was much longer than the other. I prayed:

> In the name of Jesus, I curse the spirit of trauma and fear that entered this body from so many years ago. I curse this arthritis, in Jesus' name. Father, I command all the vertebrae and discs to go into place. I command all that bruising that happened years ago to be gone, all the pain to go, and the leg to grow, in Jesus' name. Thank You, Jesus.

Smiling, she reported the pain was gone and her legs were equal. She said, "I actually started to feel something as soon as I stepped up here." Praise God. Just walking forward with faith that God would touch her and heal her problem started the healing process.

Sciatica

The sciatic nerve runs down the spinal cord to the buttocks and legs. Various conditions can trigger compression or injury of the sciatic nerve, causing pain, numbness, or tingling to travel down the hip and leg. Check the length of the person's legs. If one leg is shorter than the other, pray for the shorter leg to grow out. Then pray:

> Father, in the name of Jesus, I command that sciatic nerve to be released. I command all inflammation and pain to go, in Jesus' name, and for all the discs to be restored to their proper place. Thank You, Jesus.

Arthritis

Arthritis is a group of more than 100 medical conditions that affect the musculoskeletal system. Arthritis usually affects the joints of the body, causing pain, stiffness, inflammation, and damage to cartilage. As the joint cartilage wears away, the bones rub together, causing painful deformities and interfering with daily tasks such as walking, climbing stairs, keyboarding, or just using a knife and fork.

Some forms of arthritis can damage the heart, lungs, kidneys, blood vessels, or other parts of the body. While the most common form—osteoarthritis—usually affects people over 60, arthritis can strike at any age. The following prayer for osteoarthritis can be used for most forms of arthritis, with slight modifications.

Osteoarthritis

Osteoarthritis is a chronic inflammation and wearing down of the joints that causes pain with movement. After prayer, have the person check his back by touching his toes or making other movements that were difficult or painful before the prayer. Pray:

> *Father, in the name of Jesus, I curse this osteoarthritis. I command any bone spurs to be dissolved. I command it all to go and for all inflammation to leave. I command new cartilage, the healing of every joint in this body, in Jesus' name. Thank You, Jesus.*

Osteoarthritis, the most common form of knee arthritis, is a degenerative joint disease.

Osteopenia or Osteoporosis

> *Father, in the name of Jesus, I curse this osteopenia (or osteoporosis). I break any generational curses of osteopenia or osteoporosis. I speak the absorption of enough calcium and Vitamin D and the rebuilding of the density of every bone in this body*

to normal healthy levels. I command this spine to straighten, in Jesus' name. Thank You, Jesus.

As the Holy Spirit leads, pray a prayer of repentance with the person. The Word of God links sin with bone disease: *"There is no soundness in my flesh because of Your anger, nor any health in my bones because of my sin"* (Ps. 38:3). Likewise, *"Fear the Lord and depart from evil. It will be health to your flesh, and strength to your bones"* (Prov. 3:7b-8).

Breaking word curses may also be necessary. *"Pleasant words are like a honeycomb, sweetness to the soul and health to the bones"* (Prov. 16:24).

Shoulder and Rotator Cuff Injuries

The muscles and tendons in the shoulder are part of a structure called the rotator cuff. They connect the upper arm bone to the shoulder blade and secure it to the shoulder socket. Tearing or bruising these muscles and tendons by a fall, heavy lifting, or repetitive overhead arm action can cause severe pain, weakness, and a restricted range of motion. It is often difficult and painful for people to raise the affected arm or to sleep on that side. Bursitis occurs when the fluid-filled sacs, or bursas, which cushion the shoulder joint, become inflamed.

Prayer for Rotator Cuff Injuries

Lay your hands on the person's shoulder(s). Then pray:

I command any tendonitis or inflammation of the bursa to go, in the name of Jesus, and I speak healing and restoration to any strain, sprains, or tears. I command all pain and weakness to go and for complete range of motion to be restored. I speak a new rotator cuff, in Jesus' name. Thank You, Jesus.

Shoulder Pain

Do not give up when a person's pain does not leave immediately. Persevere. Don't forget to pray against trauma so the person receives total healing.

A man came forward for prayer for his shoulder. He did not know the cause of the injury. He simply knew it was painful and he did not have good range of motion.

I prayed: *"Father, in the name of Jesus, I speak a whole new shoulder. I command all the pain to go, and I command these ribs to go back into place, in Jesus' name. Say thank You, Jesus."*

His pain was still present. I continued, *"Father, in the name of Jesus, I command the rest of that pain to go. I command all the cartilage, tendons, and muscles to go back into their proper place and all inflammation to go, in Jesus' name. Thank You, Jesus. How does that feel?"*

He admitted there was a difference, but the pain had not gone away. I added: *"One more thing. Father, in the name of Jesus, I command the trauma to leave this shoulder. Say thank You, Jesus."*

He responded, "Thank You, Jesus. The pain is gone!"

Carpal Tunnel Syndrome

Carpal tunnel syndrome is a painful condition of the hands and fingers caused by pressure on the hand's major nerve in a small passageway—or tunnel—through the carpal bones that form the wrist. Symptoms can include numbness, tingling, burning, weakness, and pain. It can be caused by fluid retention or repetitive motion, such as computer keyboarding or playing the piano with the wrong technique. Other causes are rheumatoid arthritis, diabetes, or thyroid problems.

For people who use the computer regularly, the proper hand position and office furniture arrangement can help prevent carpal tunnel syndrome. If you type on computer keyboards frequently or do other repetitive hand and finger motion, pray over your carpal tunnels regularly, and command them to function properly and the blood to flow normally through the hands and fingers. When you pray for someone with carpal tunnel syndrome, lay hands on the wrist area and command the muscles to relax; for the pain, numbness, and tingling to go; and for normal circulation to be restored. If the person has other contributing causes, such as arthritis, command that to go.

When testing for carpal tunnel syndrome, I ask the person to put her pinky finger and thumb together as tightly as she can. I attempt to pull the two digits apart by pulling against them with my index finger. If the person has a normal level of strength, I can't separate the thumb and finger, but when carpal tunnel is present, separation of the digits is easy. Along with loss of strength, carpal

tunnel causes tingling in the fingers and/or numbness, particularly at night. The symptoms can be in both wrists, but it can be present in just one.

Father, in the name of Jesus, I command these carpal tunnels to open up, and for all tendons, muscles, and ligaments to return to the proper length and strength. I command all pain, tingling, and numbness to go and for proper circulation to be restored, in Jesus' name. Thank You, Jesus.

After prayer, I test the strength of the person's hand again with the pinky and thumb pressed against one another. Once the person is healed, the strength will return and the pain is gone.

Pelvic Misalignment

If someone is pigeon-toed or has duck feet, the pelvic area is out of alignment. Pray:

In the name of Jesus, I command the pelvic area to go into alignment and the feet to go in the proper direction.

For flat feet, also pray for the arches to return to their proper position.

RENAL, KIDNEYS, AND BLADDER IRREGULARITIES

Kidney Failure

Kidney failure can develop as a complication of high blood pressure or diabetes as well as cancer, stones, or repeated infections. The kidneys primarily function as a filter to dispose of impurities and excess fluid from the blood. These by-products of digestion are sent to the bladder to exit the body. When a kidney loses its ability to do its job, impurities build up and the body becomes toxic. Without treatment such as dialysis or a kidney transplant, the body will die.

Father, I rebuke the curse of trauma and pain. I curse the stones that have developed within the kidneys. I command the scar tissue caused by kidney stones to be healed and for the kidneys to function normally in Jesus' name.

Incontinence

Incontinence can occur at any age. It usually develops in later years with loss of control of the bladder or bowels. Women who have had children are particularly susceptible due to the stretching of the lower abdominal structures during pregnancy and delivery.

Men can have uncontrolled incontinence after prostate removal. If they have difficulty passing urine, the problem can be an enlarged prostate, which is common in later years.

Father, I speak this pelvis to go back to perfect alignment. I speak a new bladder with normal function. I speak strength to abdominal and pelvic muscles to control all episodes of incontinence in Jesus' name.

Enlarged Prostate

The prostate is a small gland near the neck of the bladder that produces seminal fluid. An enlarged prostate, which may develop as men age, can interfere with testosterone production as well as a smooth urinary flow. An enlarged prostate and erectile dysfunction are common problems for which you may be asked to pray. Lay hands on yourself, or have the person for whom you are praying lay his hand on his lower abdomen.

Father, I curse the spirit of trauma and stress. I curse it and command it to leave in Jesus' name. I pray for this pelvis area to come into alignment and the prostate to return to its normal size and function. I speak a new prostate gland into this body. Hormones, come into perfect harmony and balance and function normally in Jesus' name. Thank You, Jesus, for Your goodness and healing of this situation.

If the man has prostate cancer, add:

I curse the cancer and every prion in this man's body. I curse the spirit of death and speak complete restoration of his hormone balance and a new, cancer-free prostate gland, in Jesus' name.

When a man is healed, pray for the restoration of hormone balance for his wife as well. She may have to readjust to a new level of marital intimacy as her husband's drive and vitality are restored.

Pain

Headaches and Migraines

Headaches can cause pressure and tightness in the head that sometimes extends into the neck. Some headaches feel like a tight band around the head while others cause sharp pain on one side of the head near an eye.

Migraines are chronic headaches that may be accompanied by severe pain, nausea, vomiting, dizziness, and sensitivity to light or sound. Most migraines are caused by stress, but sometimes they are the result of not eating properly or getting enough sleep. Migraines are occasionally caused by a generational curse. They can also result from a traumatic event, trying to perform too hard, losing someone you love, a death, or a move.

When praying for the healing of a headache or migraine, put your hand on your own head if you are praying for yourself, or on the head of the person you are praying for, and say:

Some headaches feel like a tight band around the forehead. Pray for yourself or others by placing your hand around that area.

Father, in the name of Jesus, I send the word of healing to _____ and I command the headache(s) to go in Jesus' name. I command the blood vessels to dilate properly, allowing the blood to flow through this body freely, and I command every bit of pain to leave, in Jesus' name.

If the pain is going but is not completely gone, continue with: *In the name of Jesus, I command the rest of it to go. Thank You, Jesus.*

While the above prayer deals with the physical symptoms of a headache or migraine, God may reveal a deeper issue to you. If He does, ask the person about it and deal with the root cause of the headaches.

A woman came to me for ministry. She had been experiencing migraines after a broken heart had opened the door to a spirit of self-hatred. That spirit needed to be removed before her healing could be complete. The Holy Spirit will give you words of knowledge and discernment about underlying roots and hidden needs. Remain open to His voice.

The headaches had started five years before. She admitted she had experienced a serious traumatic event at 18 to 20 years of age which broke her heart. She was divorced.

God showed me that the situation broke her heart and opened the door to depression. It also brought on the migraines and feelings of worthlessness and rejection. There had been a lot of pain and shame about the situation.

I comforted her with the words, "God is going to set you completely free right now."

Father, in the name of Jesus, I curse the spirits of trauma, fear, rejection, abandonment, abuse, and shame. I speak to those spirits of hopelessness, depression, and oppression that have been hanging over this life like a cloud the past several years.

The heaviness of that curse is now broken off, and the stress and migraines that came with it are cursed and commanded to go, in Jesus' name. No more migraines and no more pain in this heart, in Jesus' name. Father, I speak peace from the top of her head to the soles of her feet, a waterfall of peace. Thank You, Jesus.

She then repeated the following prayer after me:

In Jesus' name, I renounce the words spoken against me. I am lovely. I am loving. Father, I thank You for giving me another opportunity to really love somebody without fear. Thank You, Jesus. Amen.

Once the words were spoken, her entire countenance changed and the dark cloud disappeared. Her face and eyes brightened remarkably.

Pain of Other or Nonspecific Areas

I curse the pain (and or the spirit of pain). I command it to leave, in Jesus' name.

FIBROMYALGIA

Fibromyalgia is characterized by widespread muscular pain, tender points in the body that react to firm pressure, and chronic fatigue. Some people may also experience memory loss or sleep problems, numbness or tingling in the extremities, depression, and headaches or migraines. Although its cause is unknown, fibromyalgia often follows a traumatic experience. Trauma triggers the release of destructive stress hormones and leads to hopelessness, depression, and chronic fatigue syndrome. The body's hormones and electrical and magnetic frequencies get out of balance.

For many years, fibromyalgia was considered a psychological problem and treated as such. Slowly, it was recognized and started being treated as a disease process of its own. The medical community may never understand how or why it occurs, but those who suffer with the disability will attest to its existence with tears running down their cheeks.

Get to the Root

A woman received prayer for fibromyalgia and made moderate progress toward healing, but never dealt with the root cause. As a result, she was still experiencing pain. Without getting rid of the cause, the disease may return, and, in her case, the root was trauma.

Trauma and stress can affect your body, emotions, and behavior. The release of stress hormones is the body's natural response to danger—the "fight or flight" response that protects you in an emergency. When a threat looms, the hypothalamus signals to the adrenal glands to release adrenaline, cortisol, and other hormones. As a result, the heart rate increases, the blood pressure rises, blood sugar levels rise, and a spurt of energy and alertness heightens your response to an emergency. The stress hormones also suppress the immune and digestive systems and other areas of the body not necessary in an emergency.

When the danger has passed, the body's hormone levels return to normal. If the stress is constant or long-term, as is common in our society, the constant surge of hormones can disrupt many bodily functions and lead to disease.

When you pray for diseases such as fibromyalgia, you must pray against trauma and stress. If the person is experiencing pain in a specific area, pray for that as well.

Fibromyalgia

Father, in the name of Jesus, I curse the spirits of trauma, stress, and fear. I command them to leave. I also curse the spirits of fibromyalgia, pain, chronic fatigue, and hopelessness, in Jesus' name. I speak health and wholeness to this body and I command all pain to go. I command the chemicals, pH balance, and the electromagnetic frequencies in this body to return to perfect harmony and balance.

I speak a completely restored immune system, in Jesus' name. I command the spirit of rejection and all pain that has settled and made a home in this person to leave. This is an eviction notice. Father, in the name of Jesus, I thank You for completely healing _____ of fibromyalgia, stress, and all pain. Thank You, Jesus.

POWER PRAYERS OVER DEATH AND CANCER

The Feeding Frenzy Stops Here

When I traveled down the Amazon River with my parents, we could hear the bumping of snakes and the thumping of piranhas against our boat. We heard eerie, scary sounds. Piranhas are ferocious, carnivorous fish with razor-sharp teeth that tear the flesh off their prey. A school of piranhas can chew up a human in seconds.

On that trip, someone gave my father a set of piranha teeth, and he put them on his desk when he got home. Those jaws weren't scary at all sitting on my dad's desk, but they reminded me of the cancer that had tried to eat my flesh. If you take something out of its natural environment and put it in a controlled environment, it will die.

Your responsibility includes taking the food from the piranhas that attempt to devour your body, soul, mind, or spirit. These destructive forces feed on anger, unforgiveness, bitterness, resentment, and unbelief. Some people, even doctors, tell cancer patients, "You just have to learn to live with it." No!

That is not true. You have to take authority over the piranhas in your life.

Cancer is an abnormal cell growth that spreads by uncontrolled cell division. It can invade nearby tissue or spread to other parts of the body via the blood and lymphatic systems. Although there are several types of cancer, they all have one thing in common: they absorb and transform your flesh and cells. Root causes that are not dealt with open the door for cancer to attack your body and feed like piranhas on your flesh. Put those razor-sharp teeth into a controlled environment through repentance, obedience, and faith in the power of God to set you free once and for all. Declare your home, your church, and the 4 corners of your world a cancer-free zone, in Jesus' name.

I am tired of the enemy giving people cancer. I am appalled when people say that God gave them cancer to teach them a lesson. God does not even have cancer to give. God gives life, blessings, joy, and peace. His precious gifts do not include death, sickness, or pain.

God will fight the battle for you by reversing the enemy's attacks (see Exod. 14:14). What the enemy tries to put on you, a child of God, will boomerang back onto him. He will be very sorry he ever attacked you.

I know he is sorry for what he did to me and to my family because God is now using me to set people free. *"Therefore if the Son makes you free, you shall be free indeed"* (John 8:36).

The following prayers are examples of how to pray for people with a diagnosis of cancer.

Breast Cancer

Father, in the name of Jesus, I curse this breast cancer and I curse the spirit of death. I command it to be gone, in Jesus' name. I curse all the prions in this body. I command all the

lymph nodes to be completely free of cancer and I speak a healthy new breast, in Jesus' name.

Breast Cancer and Lymphoma

Father, in the name of Jesus, I curse this cancer and every prion in this body, and I command it all to go. I curse the spirit of death, in Jesus' name. And in the name of Jesus, I speak two new breasts. This is the year of restoration. The Word of God says, "Ye have not, because ye ask not" (James 4:2 KJV). I will not limit God. Jesus said, "If you ask anything in My name, I will do it" (John 14:14). I speak restoration of every damaged cell within this body to complete healthy function. Thank You, Jesus.

Lung Cancer

Father, in the name of Jesus, I curse the cancer of the lungs, and I curse the spirit of death. I curse every prion in this body and I speak healthy new lungs, in Jesus' name.

Colon Cancer

I curse this cancer, in Jesus' name, not only in the colon, but also throughout this body. I curse every prion and command the spirit of death to go, and I speak a new colon installed and functioning properly, and no cancer, in Jesus' name. Thank You, Jesus.

Cancer of the Blood

Father, I curse the spirit of cancer and I command it to be gone, in Jesus' name. I speak a supernatural blood transfusion and Holy Ghost fire to purge and purify this blood of all cancer, in Jesus' name. I curse every prion in this body and I command them all to leave, in Jesus' name. I curse the spirits of

trauma, fear, and death, and I command them to be gone, in Jesus' name. Thank You, Jesus.

Bone Cancer

Father, in the name of Jesus, I curse this cancer and every prion in this body. In Jesus' name, I curse the spirit of trauma and fear, and I curse the spirit of death. I speak a whole new skeletal system, in Jesus' name. Thank You, Jesus.

Bone Marrow

Father, in the name of Jesus, I curse the spirit of trauma and fear. I command it to be gone. I curse this cancer and I curse the spirit of death. I speak health and wholeness and a supernatural bone marrow transplant, healthy bones, and healthy blood, in Jesus' name. Thank You, Jesus.

Reaction to Treatment

Father, in the name of Jesus, I curse any damage that the chemotherapy (and/or radiation, medicine, or surgery) has caused, and I speak health, wholeness, and restoration to this body, in Jesus' name. Thank You, Jesus.

Widespread Cancer

A woman came to a meeting directly from the hospital. She had cancer of the breast, bone, and liver. In addition, she had just had a metal hip replacement because cancer had infiltrated her hip.

I told her, "You sound like the woman with the issue of blood. It wasn't convenient for her to go to Jesus for healing, but through all her pain, she endured until she found Him. May God bless the people who helped get you here because I don't think you could have gotten here by yourself. God is going to honor your faith."

Father, in the name of Jesus, I curse the spirit of trauma and the spirit of fear, in Jesus' name, and I command it to go. I curse the spirit of cancer and the spirit of death, and every prion in this body, in Jesus' name. For any damage that this cancer has caused in this body, I speak complete restoration of every organ and bone, including the hip that just got replaced. The doctors will say, "I thought we replaced this." You did, but this one is bone, not metal. And Father, I curse any damage that chemotherapy or radiation has caused. I speak a new breast, a new liver, and health and wholeness throughout all of these bones and organs, in Jesus' name. Thank You, Jesus.

If you pray for anyone diagnosed with cancer, including yourself, also pray for the spirit of trauma to leave. I was praying for a man who had been ill with cancer of the spine for 11 years, when the Holy Spirit revealed to me that he had suffered a trauma about 11 years before, a painful divorce. We prayed against the spirits of trauma and of cancer and the man was healed.

Christ—The Big "C" Versus cancer: the Little "c"

Many people think that cancer is the big "C," but that is not true. Cancer is the little "c" because Christ is the big "C." He is greater and more powerful than any disease, including cancer.

As mentioned earlier, when I was first diagnosed with breast cancer, I saw it as a way out of the suffering and pain I was going through at the time. As I looked at that sonogram screen filled with cancer, I realized I had to choose life for the sake of my girls. I said, "Father, in the name of Jesus, I am going to live and not die and declare the works of the Lord. I choose life! The doctors spoke death over me, but I choose life!" God completely healed me. And He can heal you, too.

If you pray for someone with cancer, place your hand on his or her chest over the person's heart, and pray:

Father, in the name of Jesus, I curse the spirit of trauma and fear that has come into _____ life and body. I cut off that spirit of death, in Jesus' name. The curse of death that has been spoken over _____ is now cut off, in Jesus' name.

Tell the person to repeat: *I shall live and not die and declare the works of the Lord. I choose life. I choose life. I shall live and not die and declare the works of the Lord. I choose life! Amen!*

Father, I curse this cancer that has attacked this body. I speak a new body part (insert the body part affected) *into this body. I speak complete healing and restoration to any tissue or cells that have been damaged by surgery, treatments, or medicines. Normal function is returned in Jesus' name.*

Root Causes

Follow the Arrows—Surprise

Some ministry can begin as healing prayer but develop into much more as the Holy Spirit gives words of knowledge about other needs. You must be sensitive to and wait on the Holy Spirit's leading.

A woman who I will call JoBeth came for ministry. She was tired of fighting with sugar diabetes, high blood pressure, and arthritis. She was more than ready to get rid of it all. God gave me the words to pray. He showed me JoBeth had a lot of grief and loss in her life.

Father, I curse the spirit of trauma, fear, grief, abandonment, and betrayal, and I command all that to go, in Jesus' name. I command all the pain to go in Jesus' name. Thank You, Jesus.

Even her son who stood nearby was surprised to see the tears that started flowing. JoBeth had spent years being strong for her family and was feeling the effects of the stress. I continued to minister.

In the name of Jesus, I command this blood pressure to return to normal. I curse the arthritis and command it to go. I curse the diabetes and I command it to be gone. I speak a new pancreas, in Jesus' name. I speak peace from the top of your head to the soles of your feet. I speak strength and wholeness into

these legs, in Jesus' name. I curse any form of neuropathy and I command that to be gone. I speak restoration, total restoration.

God gave me a word of knowledge. Someone had stolen something very valuable from JoBeth, but she had never told anyone but God.

I told her, "Through the years you said, 'If I only had that money.' Now you're going to say: 'When I get the money....' And it's not going to come back dollar for dollar. It's going to come back sevenfold because that's the kind of God we serve. You never held it against that person. You just asked God to bless that person in spite of the betrayal you experienced. God saw your heart, and He's going to bless you."

I then turned to the son. "I believe your mother was betrayed by someone you know. She didn't want you to hold anything against that person so she kept it inside to save you from hurting your relationship with that person. I know you would protect your mother and not allow anyone to mess with your mom. This experience shows she has a pure heart. It also shows that God has heard her cries all these years, and He determined to share something that only she, God, and the other person knew. God revealed it now to bless her."

Ministry to this woman is a good example of what to do as you pray for someone. Listen to the person and to the Holy Spirit. I listened and followed the arrows from the symptoms of the disease to what God wanted to do in her life.

As you wait, God may tell you something that no one else knows. God wanted to bring this information out into the open and help her deal with it. Follow the Holy Spirit to the solution. Listen to His promptings. He will direct you.

FEAR AND ANXIETY

I sought the Lord, and He heard me, and delivered me from all my fears (Psalm 34:4).

Fear is the opposite of trust and faith in Jesus Christ. When Peter got out of the boat in a storm and began to walk on the water toward Jesus:

> *...he saw that the wind was boisterous, he was afraid; and beginning to sink he cried out, saying, "Lord, save me!" And immediately Jesus stretched out His hand and caught him, and said to him, "O you of little faith, why did you doubt?"* (Matthew 14:30-31)

It's interesting to read what happened when that fishing boat reached the other side of the lake. First came the storm, the battle, then the victory and the miracle!

> *When they had crossed over, they came to the land of Gennesaret. And when the men of that place recognized Him, they sent out into all that surrounding region, brought to Him all who were sick, and begged Him that they might only touch the hem of His garment. And as many as touched it were made perfectly well* (Matthew 14:34-36).

Jesus sets you free from all fear because He is full of love, mercy, and compassion for you. But He also sets you free so that you can minister freedom and healing to others. Remember, the next time a challenge or mountain stands in front of you, something great is on the other side. He helps you through the experience into victory.

Instead of sliding into fear and anxiety, start praising God for what is coming right around the corner. Build your faith on His Word rather than feeding your fears with the doom and gloom of the world's philosophy. Praise Him!

Close Encounter With an Alligator

When I was six years of age, my best friend's family owned the Miami Serpentarium in Miami, Florida. Her parents kept serpents and other reptiles there, from turtles to alligators. One day when we were playing in her home just behind the Serpentarium, a 12-foot alligator got loose from the pit and started slithering through the house. It tried to go through the kitchen into the bedroom where we were playing. Although the alligator eventually was subdued and returned to its pit, this terrifying and traumatic experience left a vivid impression on my mind and emotions.

Fifty years later, I returned to Florida for a booksellers' convention in Orlando. A security guard approached my group and said, "I want you to be aware that there's an alligator on the floor." I knew that in some parts of Florida it is not uncommon for alligators to get loose. My demeanor changed.

I continued to communicate with the influential, powerful booksellers, keeping one eye on the person talking to me while the other scanned the floor for an alligator on the move. I knew I couldn't run as fast as I could when I was six, so I was ready to run or hide behind someone. The entire time I was talking, fear escalated within me. I fully expected an alligator was about to come out from under a table set up nearby. Even though I had been healed of the childhood trauma, the possibility of a reoccurrence was frightening.

Ultimately, the wayward alligator was found and recaptured. It was four to five-feet long and its mouth was taped shut. The security guard had not told us the whole story— the alligator was a marketing strategy to draw people to one of the exhibits.

Here is a photo of me holding the alligator. As I was holding it, fear started overwhelming me. I quickly prayed, "In the name of Jesus, I command the spirit of trauma and fear to go." That fear had to obey my words, so it left while I was still holding the alligator.

Notice how I dealt with this fear: My instinct was to run, but I did not. I overcame my fear by facing it head-on, in the name of Jesus. Choose not to give in to a spirit of fear. Go after the things that you once feared the most and overcome fear and trauma forever.

"Therefore if the Son makes you free, you shall be free indeed" (John 8:36).

Break the Bonds of Fear and Anxiety

During a healing service, a woman I will call Anne Marie came to the podium for prayer. The entire time that I was ministering to Anne Marie, she couldn't take her eyes off her husband, who was sitting in the third row. I had to ask her to pay attention to me so she could be set free.

She had been married for more than 40 years, but was agoraphobic (having an irrational fear of being in public or in open spaces). For all those years Anne Marie had suffered severe anxiety attacks whenever her husband went to work and left her alone. She was oppressed by the fear that he would never come home. Because she was trapped in that horrible prison, she kept looking at her husband to make sure he had not left her alone at the meeting.

Even when Anne Marie went to a restroom, he would have to stay outside to communicate with her, "I'm out here. I'll see you in a few minutes. Don't worry, I am right here." Experiencing such fear, crying, and pleading, "Don't leave me, don't leave me" was equally horrible for the husband as well. She couldn't leave the house or drive a car because she was too terrified to go anywhere without him.

Even as I started praying against the spirit of trauma, all she could focus on was her irrational fear that he was going to leave her. She couldn't comprehend that if he hadn't left in more than 40 years, he wasn't going to leave now. I prayed against the spirit of trauma, anxiety, and fear. It all left.

Father, I curse the spirit of trauma, anxiety, and fear. It has to leave. I speak health, peace, faith, God-confidence, and love into this situation in Jesus' name.

A few months later we were back in the area. Anne Marie shared her testimony. Her husband had asked her to go to a store and get a newspaper early one morning. She drove to the store, but it hadn't opened for business yet. She was sitting in the car by herself when someone else drove up. She not only got out of the car to talk to the person, Anne Marie also prayed for the woman and she was healed. The store opened, Anne Marie bought the newspaper, and was on her way home when she suddenly realized, "Oh, God, I really am healed." At that moment, she realized that she was finally free from fear.

Notice that after this woman was set free from fear, she was then free to serve God and pray for the healing of others. When Zacharias, the father of John the Baptist, was filled with the Holy Spirit, he prophesied:

Blessed is the Lord God of Israel, for He has visited and redeemed His people....To grant us that we, being delivered from the hand of our enemies, might serve Him without fear, in holiness and righteousness before Him all the days of our life (Luke 1:68,74-75).

REJECTION

A young woman, whom I will call Joy, came for prayer. The Holy Spirit revealed that she had been deeply wounded by rejection. Her wound was complicated by the fact that she blamed herself for her parents' divorce many years before. Her parents were still alive. Even the thought of speaking to them made her feel sick. Their relationship was very tenuous.

Gently, I told her, "You love them and that is why you are hurt. They couldn't hurt you if you didn't care. It's better to love and take the chance of being hurt again than to put up the walls of division. Those walls you build brick by brick trap you inside."

First, I led the woman in a prayer of forgiveness. After she forgave those who had hurt her, we confronted the root—her reaction to her parents' divorce, which opened the door for the spirit of rejection to enter and become a stronghold in her life.

A hurting person often shoulders the blame for the situation whether or not he or she was the cause. A key question to ask after such a trauma is simply: "What did you do to make this happen?" When the person stops to think about it, he or she usually realizes that the false guilt is irrational.

This often occurs with young children who blame themselves for their parents breakup and divorce. Parents can also lash out in anger at the child because they don't want to accept their own responsibility for the failed marriage. Rejection can hang on and affect people throughout their lifetime if not dealt with properly.

Rejection can occur at any age. Relationships are lost or destroyed. Divorces, fights, misunderstandings...words said in anger or pain can destroy years of friendship and love. The enemy will use every weapon he has to wreck families and destroy marriages.

Prayer of Forgiveness

Father, my parents were not perfect, but they have been good parents. They have said and done things that hurt me. I forgive them and I ask You to separate those sins from my parents and put them on the cross, never to be held against them again. Bless my parents, in Jesus' name.

Father, I forgive _____ for hurting me. Take this sin from _____ and put it on the cross, never to be held against _____ again, in Jesus' name. Father, bless _____. Father, forgive me and cleanse me from anger and resentment against anyone who has hurt or rejected me. Thank You, Jesus.

You or the person you are praying for may need to pray the last portion of this prayer using all the names of people who have hurt you or him.

Get to the Root

Sue, I will call her, believed she was a failure. "My parents and stepmother wanted to get rid of me because I was a disappointment to them. I didn't become what they wanted me to be. I didn't go to the school they wanted. I'm overweight. I don't live where they want me to live."

She had no answers when I asked, "What did you do at 12 years of age to make them want to get rid of you? What can a 12-year-old girl do to deserve that?" She cried. I went on, "You have been beating yourself up since you were 12 because you thought you were a horrible little girl. The enemy wants you to believe that your parents' divorce was your fault, but there's nothing a little 12-year-old girl could have done to make this happen. You've blamed yourself for not being what your parents wanted. Do you think that's really the truth? The truth is, you have been believing a lie."

I told her to repeat the following positive affirmations after me. Through tears, she obeyed.

"I've been believing a lie. I'm not going to blame myself anymore for not meeting their expectations. I love _____ (insert the name of the person receiving ministry). I am a good girl (or boy). I am worthy to be loved by my parents. I am worthy to be loved by God."

Then I had Sue continue with the following prayer:

Father, I take all the responsibility and guilt for my parents' divorce and I release it to You and put it on Your altar, never to trouble me again, in Jesus' name. I renounce this false responsibility. Their divorce was not my fault. I believed a lie. I have believed a lie. I have been believing a lie! Jesus, You were rejected so we don't have to be or feel rejected. I lay all this rejection and pain on Your altar and release it to You. Father, I receive Your love for me, in Jesus' name. Thank You, Jesus.

As the woman released the burden she had been carrying to the Lord, she was slain in the Spirit. When she finally got up, she was smiling and her face was glowing. She was a new woman.

When my father and my mother forsake me, then the Lord will take care of me (Psalm 27:10).

IMMUNITY FROM WITHIN: STRESS AND THE ADRENAL GLANDS

Trauma and Stress

Trauma and stress help open the door to sickness because they attack and weaken the immune system. The immune system is the body's defense network—the organs, cells, and tissues that protect it from bacteria, viruses, parasites, toxins, fungi, and other foreign invaders. The immune system's first line of defense is to repel invading organisms. If that fails, it launches a coordinated search and destroy mission. In an autoimmune disease, the immune system mistakenly attacks the body's healthy cells or tissue. For example, in rheumatoid arthritis the immune system attacks the joints as if they were foreign bodies. Allergies occur when the immune system reacts strongly to an allergen. People who receive organ transplants need prayer for their immune systems not to attack the new organ and that any drugs given to minimize this risk will not weaken the immune system's defense against infections.

The immune system also attacks prions—infectious pathogens that cause degenerative diseases of the brain and nervous system.[1] Some diseases caused by prions are hereditary and require prayer against generational curses.

To maintain a healthy immune system, it is important to keep your body in alignment electrically, magnetically, and chemically, and with the proper pH balance of the body's alkaline and acid levels. Stress can cause the body's pH to get out of balance. This imbalance not only weakens the body and opens the door to disease, but it also can hinder the ability to get pregnant.

One way to protect your immune system is to learn how to manage stress. Physical and psychological stress is part of everyday life, but some people internalize stress or carry it unnecessarily. Consistent stress weakens the immune system and releases stress hormones. It can lead to heart disease, sleep and digestive problems, memory loss, and other health issues.[2] When people with weakened immunity are exposed to a contagious disease, they are more likely to become infected.

So it's important that you keep your immune system strong with a healthy physical and spiritual lifestyle. When your immune system is strong, you'll pray for sick people and you will not get sick. Stay trauma and stress free, and no matter what is in your genealogy or who is coughing around you, you can walk in divine health.

Adrenal Glands

The adrenals are two tiny but powerful glands that sit above the kidneys. They affect your energy, endurance, and quality of life. They work with the hypothalamus and pituitary gland to produce hormones that control the metabolism of fats, proteins, and carbohydrates, minimize inflammation and allergic reactions, and regulate the metabolism, immune system, sexual characteristics, and blood pressure and chemistry, including blood sugar levels. The outer layer, or adrenal cortex, releases corticosteroids.

A primary purpose of the adrenal glands is to help your body deal with stress and survive. When you are under stress, the core, or adrenal medulla, secretes epinephrine and norepinephrine (noradrenaline), which increases your heart rate and the blood flow to the muscles and brain. These stress hormones contribute to the "fight or flight" reaction that protects you in a threatening situation.

Adrenal gland disorders are due either to the production of too many or not enough hormones. Most doctors recognize and treat Addison's disease, which is caused by inadequate hormones produced by the cortex. However, many doctors do not give credence to or treat less extreme adrenal hormone deficiencies. Your knowledge of how the adrenal glands work will help you pray with focus for yourself or others who may be suffering from low levels of these essential hormones.

Adrenal Fatigue

The most common prayer request related to the adrenal glands is due to stress-related adrenal fatigue. Some people may not specifically ask for prayer for their adrenal glands. They may complain about their symptoms without realizing what is causing them.

Chronic stress, poor nutrition, and intensely negative emotions such as anger, bitterness, resentment, or constant fretting can cause adrenal insufficiency by decreasing the hormone production. The results are fatigue, depression, anxiety, confusion, loss of motivation, low blood pressure, forgetfulness and foggy thinking, decreased productivity, and trouble sleeping. Adrenal fatigue can open the door to fibromyalgia, hypoglycemia, a weakened immune system, disruption in blood-sugar levels, arthritis, and other conditions.

How we handle our emotions and the stress of everyday life can protect or weaken our adrenal function. For example, the Word of God offers guidance for protecting ourselves from the ravages of anxiety and fear, a contributor to the depletion of adrenal hormones:

> *Rest in the Lord, and wait patiently for Him; do not fret because of him who prospers in his way, because of the man who brings wicked schemes to pass. Cease from anger, and forsake wrath; do not fret—it only causes harm* (Psalm 37:7-8).

Prayer for Adrenal Burnout

When you pray for yourself or someone who has adrenal fatigue, place your hands on the person's back just above the kidneys, about an inch below the lowest rib. Lead the person in a prayer of repentance for any worry, fear, anxiety, anger, or holding on to stress, and not resting in the Lord or getting enough physical rest and sleep.

> *Father, in the name of Jesus, I curse all spirits of trauma, stress, worry, anxiety, and fear. They must go. I rebuke any infection or inflammation in this body, in the name of Jesus. I speak new adrenal glands and command all hormones and blood-sugar levels to return to normal levels, in Jesus' name.*

When praying for stress-related adrenal fatigue, place hands about an inch below the lowest rib.

> *Father, I repent for _____ (holding on to stress, worry, anxiety, anger, resentment, bitterness, etc.), and for not resting in You. I also repent for not making sure I get enough rest, which includes spending time with You every day, in Jesus' name. I receive Your cleansing and forgiveness. Thank You, Jesus.*

Rejoice in the Lord always. Again I will say, rejoice! ...Be anxious for nothing, but in everything by prayer and supplication, with thanksgiving, let your requests be made known to God; and the peace of God, which surpasses all understanding, will guard your hearts and minds through Christ Jesus (Philippians 4:4,6-7).

Commanding the stress to go begins your healing—turning your heart and attention to God, placing all your burdens and cares on His altar, and learning to rest and live in Him seals it. Paul concludes that quoted passage in his letter to the Philippians:

Finally, brethren, whatever things are true, whatever things are noble, whatever things are just, whatever things are pure, whatever things are lovely, whatever things are of good report, if there is any virtue and if there is anything praiseworthy— meditate on these things (Philippians 4:8).

Handling Everyday Stress

While men tend to face stress on the job, women want to be superwomen. Women think they can handle everything, fix husbands, and transform their children into angels. No one can actually fix anyone, not even him or herself. That mindset does nothing but add many layers of stress to an already hectic life.

Stress piles up, a little here and a little there. If your responsibilities and pressures are not given to God, you will be overwhelmed.

To demonstrate how this can happen, imagine a large pile of heavy books. With every issue in your life you can list, pick up a book. An imperfect marriage, uncooperative husband, children (a book for every child), teenagers (another book for each child of that age), financial difficulties, parents with health challenges, personal health issues, or a difficult job all add weight to every step you take through a long hard day. Add several books if you have lost a job or had any serious trauma in your environment.

Each heavy book represents a source of anxiety over a person or situation. You have to carry all those unstable objects while you try to clean the house, cook dinner, or pay the bills. Quite a balancing act, isn't it?

Once you realize you don't have to carry all those large heavy weights, give each "book" symbolically to God. Put each and every one of them down at His feet on His altar. You will feel the stress lift off you immediately.

The same principle applies to trauma. You may not always be able to avoid trauma, but learning to remove trauma from your own life will equip you to minister to others who have been traumatized.

When a traumatic situation resurfaces in your life, deal with it and get rid of it right away. God has given us His authority so we don't have to be victims anymore.

Father, I put _____ (insert person and/or situation) on the altar. I can't fix either the person or situation. I release this to You. I lay it on Your altar. Thank You, Jesus.

Prayer for the Immune System

Taking care of your physical body and having healthy attitudes can go a long way toward remaining in good health. Find ways to laugh, enjoy a balanced life, relax, rest, and cope properly with stress.

Pray this prayer for yourself or for others:

Father, thank You for Your gift of a strong and healthy immune system. Help me to keep my immune system strong and

functioning perfectly, the way You created it to be. I command the electrical and magnetic frequencies in my body to return to perfect harmony and balance, and the pH balance to return to normal, in Jesus' name.

Please give me wisdom in my nutrition, exercise, and sleep habits, in Jesus' name. Forgive me for lack of discipline in the area of _____. *Father, I turn over to You all the people and circumstances You have given to me. Right now I put* _____ *on the altar, in Jesus' name.* (List each relationship and situation one by one, and put each on the altar, committing them into God's care.) *Thank You, Jesus.*

REPENTANCE

If you discern any sin that needs to be confessed at any time during ministry, add a prayer of repentance. If you are struggling with unbelief regarding trust in God and faith that He is willing and able to help you, consider the father of an afflicted child, who said to Jesus:

"...if You can do anything, have compassion on us and help us." Jesus said to him, "If you can believe, all things are possible to him who believes." Immediately the father of the child cried out and said with tears, "Lord, I believe; help my unbelief!" (Mark 9:22-24)

God has compassion on us in our infirmities, and He is willing and able to strengthen, protect, and heal us. Confess any unbelief to Him and pray with faith against the ravages of stress, trauma, and disease both for yourself and for others.

Father, I repent for anything and everything I have done that was not pleasing to You. Take this sin from me and put it on the cross, never to be held against me. Help me not to sin again in Jesus' name. Thank You, Jesus. Amen.

SALVATION

Occasionally, people will come for healing just because they want their diseases removed from their body. They may not understand or care about the most important thing—salvation of their soul. Only through salvation can a person's body, soul, and spirit be totally healed and prepared for Heaven. If you have any inclination that the person coming to you for ministry has not asked Jesus into his or her heart, ask the person to pray for salvation:

Father, I repent for anything and everything I have done that was not pleasing to You. Take this sin from me and put it on the cross, never to be held against me. Help me not to sin again in Jesus' name. Jesus, come into my heart, be my Savior and Lord. Father, through Your Holy Spirit, lead me and guide me into all You have for me. Thank You, Jesus. Amen.

ENDNOTES FOR APPENDIX

1. Amanda Gardner, "Back Pain? Alternative therapies may help," CNN.com, July 24, 2010, http://www.cnn.com/2010/HEALTH/07/24/back.pain.therapies/index.html; accessed September 18, 2010. 1.

2. Stanley B. Prusiner, "Prions," abbreviated version of 1997 Nobel lecture, *PNAS*. November 10, 1998, http://www.pnas.org/content/95/23/13363.full; accessed September 18, 2010.

3. Mayo Clinic staff, "Stress: Win Control Over the Stress in Your Life," September 12, 2008, http://www.mayoclinic.com/health/stress/SR00001; accessed September 18, 2010.

SPINAL DISORDERS, MUSCLES, AND BONES

More people request prayer for back problems than for any other physical need. More than 26 million Americans between the ages of 20 to 64 suffer from ongoing back pain. It is one of the primary reasons for a visit to a doctor's office.

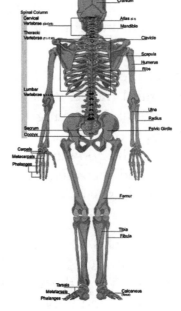

Because abnormalities with the spine and surrounding muscles, tendons and ligaments can affect so many other areas of the body, you need to understand the basic anatomy of the back and spine. In God's marvelous creation, the human body, all the individual parts must work in unity to do what they were designed to do.

The spinal column and its 31 pairs of spinal nerves is an extension of the brain, and forms the central nervous system which communicates with the rest of the body. The musculoskeletal system of the body is a very intricate design which keeps us upright and walking. The muscles, ligaments, tendons, and bones work together in amazing harmony. Few people actually understand or think about how to reach for something or how to walk across the room. The number of interwoven structures necessary for us to do the simplest things is breathtaking.

The bones which make up the spinal column are called vertebrae. These boney parts you can feel down the back of your body protect over 100,000 nerves which communicate from the brain to all areas of the human body. The brain tells every inch of the body what to do every second of life. Any interruption in this complicated electrical system causes problems with the body's function. For instance, an interruption in communication between the brain and the arm results in what we call paralysis. The arm can't move without being told what to do. This principle applies to every part of the body. Without communication to and from the brain, the body can't function. It dies.

The vertebrae also cover and protect two small tubes which carry the spinal fluid to and from the brain. As you breathe, the fluid travels up and down the spinal column bathing the nerves and allowing the necessary communication from the brain to cells of the body. Restriction of this fluid affects nerves within the body and will cause a dysfunction. If a nerve gets "pinched" between the bones, communication gets interrupted and causes pain.

The spinal column is held together by ligaments, tendons, and muscles. Ligaments connect bone to bone and tendons connect muscles to bone. Muscles move the bones of the body structure while the ligaments and tendons keep the body parts connected and moving correctly. Muscles have blood circulation and can tire with use while ligaments take much longer to heal because their circulation is minimal. A damaged ligament puts additional stress on the muscles and with injury or damage, scar tissue or adhesions can form which can contribute to additional pain.

With age, bone strength, muscle tone, and flexibility decline, making the possibility of injury or strain – and resulting pain, tingling, or numbness – more likely. When any part of the spinal column is out of alignment, a pinched nerve can cut off the proper nerve flow and disrupt the nerve's communication and control of normal function.

Certain conditions or diseases can be caused by irregularities of specific areas of the spinal column. You can better minister to someone with these symptoms if you understand some facts about the spine and central nervous system.

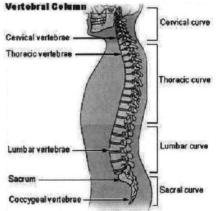

The spine is divided into the cervical (neck), dorsal (or thoracic), or lumbar (lower back) vertebrae. The discs of the spinal column act like small cushions between each vertebra (the small bones that form the backbone). These discs keep the vertebrae separated from one another and give flexibility to the spine. If a vertebra is twisted,

the misplaced disc may protrude on one side and no longer protect the other side of the vertebra. When a disc is damaged by injury, disease, or the normal wear and tear associated with aging, it can bulge or rupture. This "herniated" disc (also called "prolapsed" or "slipped" disc) pinches the nerves passing through the spine causing pain and disrupted communication between the brain and the body.

The top vertebra of the cervical spine is called the atlas and the bottom is the sacrum. The atlas connects the head with the spinal column while the sacrum is the posterior portion of the pelvic girdle and connects with the hip bones and coccyx (tail bone). The entire body rests on this weight-bearing part of your body, the five vertebra of the sacrum, which fuse together in a person's mid-teenage years.

The neck bones of the cervical vertebrae are flexible and bend very easily, thus, your head moves in many directions very easily. Damage to these seven cervical vertebrae can contribute to issues such as allergies, chronic tiredness, dizziness, ear and eye problems, fainting, headaches, high blood pressure, hoarseness, insomnia, nervousness/nervous breakdowns, neuralgia, sinus problems, sore throats, skin disorders, and stiff necks. Fractured cervical vertebrae or a "broken neck" can cause complete paralysis from the neck down which can also destroy the respiratory reflex causing death. The neck should have a natural and normal C curve. Without it, the head loses flexibility and causes neck muscle pain.

The twelve dorsal or thoracic vertebrae are all connected to the ribs which protect the heart and lungs as well as the other organs of the chest. The nerves from these relatively stationary vertebrae control the shoulders, chest, upper back, heart, lungs, gall bladder, liver, kidneys, stomach, and intestines. Damage to these nerves can cause shoulder, arm, and hand pain or numbness,

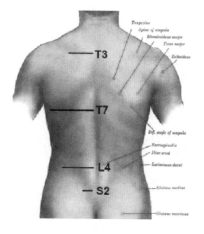

blood circulation issues, adrenal problems, pulmonary problems (lungs, throat, congestion, cough, pleurisy, asthma), fever, gall bladder problems, heart problems, hives, jaundice, shingles, stomach problems (indigestion, ulcers), and thyroid conditions.

The bottom five vertebrae of the lower back, called the lumbar vertebrae, are very vulnerable to damage or injury. Their flexibility is involved with all turning, twisting, bending, walking, and running. The nerves affected by abnormalities within these vertebrae include the abdomen (bowels, appendix, constipation, diarrhea, hemorrhoids, impotence, bladder, bed-wetting, uterus, prostate, and sterility), lower limb pain, back pain, and circulation (swelling of lower legs & varicose veins).

Short Arm or Leg

A person may appear to have either a short arm or leg when the spine and/or pelvic area are out of alignment. If a hip bone is out of place, one leg appears to be shorter than the other. 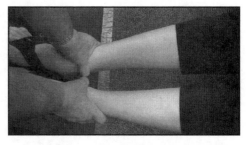 That hip bone misalignment may also cause the top rib to be out of place affecting the neck. A short leg can actually affect the body from top to bottom including the temporal bone (back of the ear), the top rib, and the lumbar vertebrae causing a pain in a knee or lower leg. Problems with bedwetting may disappear when a child has their legs grown out to release the nerves leading from the spine to the bladder. Incontinence (inability to control the passage of urine from the body) may also be helped with the same maneuver.

PRAYER FOR A SHORT LEG: *(Ask the person to sit down and stretch their legs out in front of them. While holding their ankles with your thumbs over the ankle bones, pray the following prayer.)*

Father, ligaments, muscles and tendons of this leg have caused it to draw up into a shorter position than the other leg. To walk properly, both legs need to be even. I speak to these ligaments, muscles, and tendons to relax to normal length and function normally in Jesus' name. Any other area of the body affected by this misalignment is healed and normal in Jesus' name.

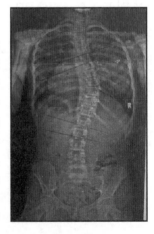

PRAYER FOR SHORT ARM: *(Ask the person to stand with feet together, facing forward with their arms extended straight out in front of them with their hands about 1 inch apart.)*

Father, ligaments, muscles, and tendons of these arms are in misalignment. Some have shortened while others have lengthened. I speak to those ligaments, muscles, and tendons of these arms to function normally and be even in Jesus' name.

Scoliosis

A person who is duck footed (feet turned outwards instead of straight ahead) or pigeon-toed (feet pointed inward), has a pelvis that is out of alignment. This misalignment affects the vertebrae and can cause a lateral curvature of the spine (scoliosis). From behind, the spine appears to be an "S". Scoliosis may also be caused by heredity or a generational curse, arthritis of the spine, or one leg being shorter than the other. It can also cause uneven shoulders, hips or waist alignment. Prayer must include the "pelvic thing".

PRAYER FOR SCOLIOSIS: *(Place hands on back / hip bones.)*

I speak to this back in Jesus' name. Every bone, muscle, ligament, and tendon in this back, you will go back into proper alignment. Those that need to grow out or stretch, do it now. Those that need to shorten, do it now. Pelvic structures, rotate back into proper position so the feet will point straight ahead in Jesus' name.

If the person has numerous problems with the spinal cord and nerves, you can add: *I speak a whole new spine into this body in Jesus' name.*

Before going any further, you need to understand why we are talking to the muscles, ligaments, and tendons and not just the bones. The muscles, ligaments, and tendons control all the bone movements which allow our bodies to function properly. Without the thousands of muscles, we would have no strength. Without the ligaments and tendons, we would not be moving any of our joints. When discussing these important body parts, the old adage "If you don't use it, you lose it!" is clearly shown in practi-

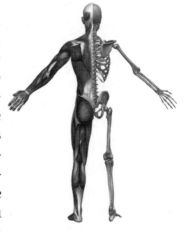

cal terms. The more you "exercise" a muscle, the stronger it gets. If you don't use a muscle, it shrinks and weakens until it is useless. Someone who has had a stroke with paralysis of an arm is a prime example. Because the arm muscles no longer receive any instructions from the brain, they don't work. Slowly, but surely, all the muscles of that limb shrink. That arm hangs limply and uselessly from the body.

Often the hand and occasionally the elbow become contractured which means the joints are locked in a bent position. Fingers cannot be straightened. With such a closed "fist" and bent elbow, putting on clothing is very difficult and cleaning these areas is a challenge. What happens to cause this? Not using the muscles. There are muscles to straighten a joint (open your hand) and opposite muscles which bend a joint (close your hand). With a constant closed hand, the muscles involved with closing your fingers shorten until you can't open your hand again. The muscles which "open" your hand stretch and can no longer pull your fingers back from the closed position.

The same principle applies to the spine. During the growth years, slumped shoulders of youngsters with poor posture don't allow normal movement of the ligaments, tendons, and muscles of the shoulders and spine. If exercise of these structures doesn't occur, poor posture will remain for life. The same thing happens with any joint that is not moved regularly. Some people who sit in a wheelchair hour after hour, month after month, year after year literally can be locked into the sitting position. When lying on their back in bed, their legs are in the air. They usually can't turn by themselves and must be turned onto one side or the other. Standing erect or walking is usually impossible.

With osteoporosis of the back, the bones become porous and weaken. As the spinal bones collapse and fuse together, the muscles on the outside that straighten the back stretch. The internal muscles that allow the body to bend over tighten. After a period of time, these muscles can't straighten or close anymore and the spine has no further flexibility. Every joint has what medically is called "range of motion". Your wrist, for example, can turn into numerous positions. However, if you don't use it (exercise it), you will lose function of your wrist. This is true about any and every joint, muscle, tendon, and ligament of the body.

Kyphosis

Kyphosis is most commonly called "hunchback". This over-curvature of the thoracic spine causes a severe rounding of the back. In young people, poor slouching posture and birth defects are contributing fac-tors. In later years, osteoporo-sis, disc degeneration, cancer of the spine, or chemotherapy can cause what is also known as a "dowager's hump". Ad-olescents who are often self-conscious have a poor body image from poor posture or

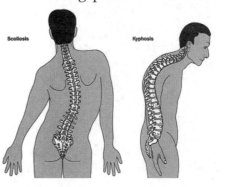

from wearing a brace to correct a more serious level of kypho-sis. Back pain caused from the spinal misalignment can be se-vere and disabling. In severe cases, the curvature of the thoracic spine causes the attached ribs to press against the lungs and heart within the chest cavity. Breathing problems can become a serious issue. Lying down or sleeping flat is severely hindered if not impossible.

PRAYER FOR KYPHOSIS *(Lay your hands on the spine/ back of the person.)*

Father, I speak to all the structures of this back. Bones, strengthen to support this body properly. Ligaments, tendons, and muscles, stretch out or shorten normally as you were de-signed to do in Jesus' name. Body, you will stand erect into

normal height for this body. Any other damage this condition may have caused is healed in Jesus' name.

Cervical Kyphosis

Cervical kyphosis is the medical diagnosis for a loss of the C (cervical) curve of the spine of the back of the neck. Fractures, trauma, injury, whiplash, arthritis, inflammation, or osteoporosis can all cause this straightening of the cervical spine.

PRAYER FOR THE "C" CURVE OF THE NECK: *(Place your fingers at the back of the neck with your thumbs in front of their ears.)*

Father, the "C" curve is not present in this cervical spine. I speak to this area of the spine. "C" curve, return to normal positioning in this neck in Jesus' name.

Whiplash can be caused by a sudden unexpected movement of the head/neck thrown backwards and then forwards. Often it occurs during an auto accident. Neck pain, swelling, decreased motion, tenderness, muscle spasms, and headaches can be symptoms of whiplash, a strain, or sprain of the muscles and ligaments of the neck (cervical spine).

PRAYER FOR WHIPLASH: *(Place your fingers at the back of the neck with your thumbs in front of their ears.)*

I curse the spirit of trauma. You have to leave this body in Jesus' name. Any pain, swelling, tenderness, muscle spasms, or headaches have to go. Full motion and function be returned now in Jesus' name.

Lordosis

Lordosis is also called "Saddleback" or "swayback". The pelvis tips forward with a marked protrusion of the stomach and deep inward curve of the spine. A large belly, pregnancy, and tight quadriceps (leg muscles) will exaggerate this condition which causes tight back muscles and pain. Tight quadriceps often occurs with long hours of sitting at a desk, at a computer, or other sedentary physical inactivity.

A certain amount of "lordosis" and "kyphosis" is normal with the various curves of the spine. The normal curvature allows balance and mobility. When these curves become accentuated or abnormal, unpleasant symptoms occur which can become very serious if untreated.

Misplaced Pelvic Area

From birth to about 20 years of age, ribs are basically cartilage, not bone. Young people lifting heavy objects can seriously affect the shape of their ribs and rib cage. During child bearing years, it is very important for women to have their pelvic area in alignment. When a baby is born, the pubic bone separates to allow the baby to pass through. If the pelvis is out of alignment, a woman will have trouble during childbirth. A misplaced pelvic area may also cause issues following pregnancy if it doesn't come back into position/alignment after birthing. This also affects the painful abdominal cramping many women endure monthly with menstruation.

PRAYER FOR WOMAN AFTER GIVING BIRTH. *(If you are a woman, place your hands on her hips while you pray. If you are a man, ask them to place their hands on their hips and you place your hands on top of theirs as you pray. You can also lay hands on yourself.)*

Father, we praise you for the miracle of birth and the new life that came forth, a precious gift from You. Now we agree that this body is going to return to normal, the pelvic bones to close, the hips to come into alignment, and all the hormones to return to normal levels. Give this precious mother all the strength, wisdom, and understanding she needs to be a good Mommy to her child in Jesus' name.

TMJ (Temporomandibular Joint)

The position of the temporal area (the bone behind the ear) is very important. 35% of all the nerve impulses which go to your brain pass through this "temporomandibular joint". The TMJ muscle, the second strongest muscle in the body, controls the jaw which means eating, swallowing, and talking are all affected by any issue with the temporal bone.

In addition, the carotid artery and autonomic nerve system (those nerves not subject to voluntary control, e.g., heart and lung activity which occur automatically with life) passes through the same TMJ area. The carotid artery carries blood 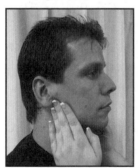 and oxygen to the brain. The nerve system travels down the back of the body to the pelvic area. Without blood and oxygen, the brain will not function. Without proper circulation of the spinal fluid, equilibrium (balance and motion) will become abnormal. Most children who have trouble walking have had an injury to the back of the head.

PRAYER FOR THE TMJ: *(Place your hands on the sides of the face with your fingers in front of the ears with fingers on the neck as you pray.)*

Father, the TMJ is very important to this person's daily activities. I speak normal function to this area with normal blood

circulation and adequate nerve communication between the brain and the body. Any symptoms or damage caused by abnormal function of this joint must go now in Jesus' name. Eating, talking, swallowing, equilibrium and any other problem are gone in Jesus' name.

Osteoporosis

Osteoporosis, osteoarthritis and crushed vertebrae or discs often result in a loss of height. According to medical information, an individual's height will not be restored. However, when God heals someone, He can restore the lost height…as we have seen many times.

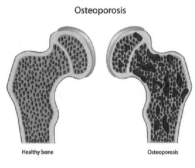

Osteoporosis

Healthy bone   Osteoporosis

In osteoporosis, the bones weaken, become porous (full of holes), fragile, and break very easily. Osteopenia, a condition which leads to osteoporosis, often begins with menopause. Calcium necessary for healthy bones may not be present in the diet so the body takes the calcium from the bones to use in more important or necessary areas of the body. Exercise and a calcium-rich diet help prevent both osteopenia and osteoporosis. There are no obvious symptoms in this silent but deadly disease. Falls or even a sudden movement can result in fractures which can leave a person helpless and prone to other complications from such immobility. For instance, even an innocent cough can cause a fractured rib that can puncture a lung, causing death. The wrong turn of a porous leg bone can become a hip fracture and leave a person wheelchair-bound. A break of a bone in the spine can cause paralysis.

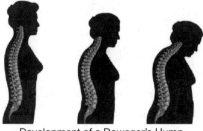

Development of a Dowager's Hump

PRAYER FOR OSTEOPOROSIS:

Father, in Jesus' name, I speak to these bones. All the weakened areas will fill in with good healthy bone and normal strength will return. Any damage or broken bones will heal and return to normal. The body will accept and use all the calcium and nutrients taken in with their diet to maintain good strength in every bone from this day forward. In Jesus' name, Amen.

Complications from Spinal Surgery

Following an injury to the spine, surgical repair may be necessary to correct a serious problem which could lead to other debilitating complications. Unfortunately, any surgery to the body will cause a certain amount of scar tissue. In the very small spaces within the spinal column and all the vertebrae, discs, and nerves, even a small amount of scar tissue can cause more constriction and additional problems. Occasionally, surgery will include fusing two or three vertebrae together. This fusion may protect the nerves and decrease pain; however, back flexibility is lost.

PRAYER FOR COMPLICATIONS AFTER SPINAL SURGERY: *(Lay hands on the back over the surgical site.)*

Father, I thank You for your marvelous creation of a spine to keep us upright. I speak to this injured back right now. Where there is scar tissue, I speak healthy normal tissue. Where there is a loss of flexibility from the fusion of the vertebrae, I speak mobility and normal movement. Furthermore, if there is any boney structure that a doctor wants to surgically repair, I speak total healing now in Jesus' name. Surgery will not be necessary because You, the ultimate Physician, will perform supernatural surgery and fix those bones right now with no hospital bills, no anesthesia, no incisions, no recovery time. Amen.

Bone Spurs

Bone spurs can appear anywhere in the body. They become a problem when they cause pain or impair function of another part of the body. For instance, a bone spur on the foot causes painful walking. A spur on the spine can pinch a nerve which causes pain in the area of the body controlled by that nerve. Bone spurs are made up of a buildup of calcium or arthritis, usually near a joint. With a calcium deficiency, the body moves calcium from the bones to other necessary areas of the body, leaving a buildup which becomes a spur. Bone spurs usually occur in later years and can be removed surgically, by laser or by improved nutrition.

PRAYER FOR BONE SPURS: *(Lay hands on area of the body reported to have bone spurs.)*

Father, the doctors say there are bone spurs causing this pain. I speak to those bone spurs in Jesus' name. Bone spurs, dissolve and disappear. Bones, you will function normally and not develop any further bone spurs. I command all pain to be gone in Jesus' name. Amen.

Arthritis

Arthritis can develop within the major or minor joints of the body, decreasing mobility and function, and most commonly develops in later years of life. Obesity, injuries, or overuse can contribute to these changes much earlier. Damage, inflammation,and bone spurs cause an abnormal buildup of bone. The cartilage protection of the joints wears out leaving bone moving on bone, causing pain. Arthritic

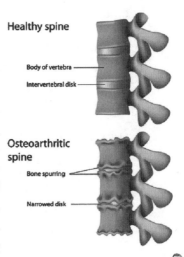

Healthy spine

Body of vertebra

Intervertebral disk

Osteoarthritic spine

Bone spurring

Narrowed disk

changes in the hands decrease strength, flexibility, and function of the fingers. It can occur in one joint at a time on either side of the body.

PRAYER FOR ARTHITIS: *(Lay hands on the affected area of the body.)*

Father, these arthritic changes in this body are hindering activity and mobility. It is difficult to be about Your business if pain and difficult walking slows a person down from responding to Your call to "GO" and "DO." I speak to all arthritis that has developed in any joint of this body. You have to go in Jesus' name. All damage, inflammation, or excessive boney deposits have to go. I speak added cartilage into the joints to protect the bones and allow full range of motion. I speak strength, flexibility, and function to every joint in this body in Jesus' name. Amen.

Rheumatoid Arthritis

Rheumatoid arthritis, an autoimmune disease, causes severe joint and bone changes and pain throughout the body, often leaving permanent deformities of the affected areas. These changes occur symmetrically – both sides of body at the same time, e.g., both hands. It is accompanied by other types of body pain also. It first develops in 20 to 40 year old adults and often requires surgery to maintain mobility of critical joints such as the hands and fingers. This very debilitating disease process can leave a person locked in bizarre positions.

PRAYER FOR RHEUMATOID ARTHRITIS: *(Lay hands on the deformities as you pray.)*

Father, this body has not functioned as you have designed. It has attacked itself and caused unpleasant changes in this body. I speak to the immune system to react and function normally. I speak to all these deformed joints to loosen up and

move normally. Rheumatoid Arthritis, you have to leave this body never to return again, in Jesus' name. Amen.

Gout

Gout is considered a form of arthritis most frequently found in the great toes. It is caused by a buildup of uric acid within the body. Usually lasting only a few days, gout causes inflammation, swelling, and severe pain to the joint. It can be related to dietary intake and triggered by an overly rich diet.

PRAYER FOR GOUTY ARTHRITIS: *(Lay hands on the affected area as you pray.)*

Father, I speak to the uric acid buildup in this body. Levels will return to normal and any damage from this inflammation must leave in Jesus' name. Gout, you have to leave this body now in Jesus' name. Pain and swelling are gone. Amen.

Bursitis

Bursitis is an inflammation of a fluid-filled sac, or bursa (like a pillow). Healthy bursae create a smooth surface for muscles and tendons to slide across bone. Shoulders, elbows, hips, and knees are the usual sites of this painful condition although, the human body has 150 of these sacs throughout the body. When bursitis occurs, movement of the inflamed area becomes difficult and painful. The symptoms can be confused with arthritis; however, bursitis is short-lived in comparison to the more permanent changes of arthritis.

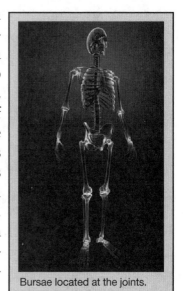
Bursae located at the joints.

PRAYER FOR BURSITIS: *(Lay hands on the affected area as you pray.)*

Father, the bursa designed to protect the muscles and tendons of this area of the body is not functioning as it should. I speak to that bursa. Inflammation and pain have to leave right now in Jesus' name. Movement will be normal and pain free in Jesus' name. Amen.

Repetitive Stress Injury

Repetitive Stress Injury syndrome includes a common list of complaints which are caused by overuse of a ligament or tendon. Tennis elbow is due to overuse of the arm causing damage to the ligament on the outer side of the arm. Carpal tunnel syndrome, swelling of the narrow channel formed by bone and ligaments, is a common problem with constant usage of the wrist (computer usage/typist or carpentry work). Cervical radiculopathy, a compression of discs in the neck can be caused by frequent holding of a telephone receiver to the ear using the shoulder. Tendonitis, often a sports injury, is an inflammation of tendons that connect bones and muscles.

PRAYER FOR REPETITIVE STRESS INJURY SYNDROME: *(Lay hands on the affected area as you pray.)*

Father, this area of the body has been used frequently and has developed inflammation and pain. I speak to the tendons and ligaments of this area. Inflammation has to leave. Pain has to leave. Any abnormality that has developed by this frequent overuse has to return to normal in Jesus' name. Amen.

Degenerative Disc Disease

Through the aging process, the discs of the spine, the shock absorbers between the bones of the spine, wear out. Named degenerative disc disease, the discs lose their fluid, thickness, and protective ability. This contributes to arthritis, bone spurs, and loss of spinal flexibility as well as chronic pain. Frequent heavy lifting and obesity increases the development of disc disease.

PRAYER FOR DEGENERATIVE DISC DISEASE: *(Lay hands on the area of affected spine if known. You can run your fingers up and down the spine if condition is generalized or site unknown.)*

Father, the discs of this spine are not doing their job. They are no longer protecting the vertebrae of the spine. I speak to these discs in Jesus' name. Discs will fill with fluid; regain thickness and protective ability to the vertebrae. Any damage caused by this degeneration, leave in Jesus' name. Spine, flexibility is returned. Any arthritic changes, bone spurs, and pain is gone. Amen.

Spondylitis and Spinal stenosis

Spondylitis (inflammation) is a form of arthritis which affects the joints of the spine. Symptoms include chronic back pain and stiffness. As these changes occur, the joints can fuse together and become immobile. A stooped over posture can be the result.

Spinal stenosis can occur if the bone deposits occur near the spinal cord. The opening designed for the nerves of the spinal cord closes or shrinks in size compressing or pinching the nerves leading to the soft tissues and organs of the body. Stenosis most commonly occurs in the vertebrae of the neck or lower back.

PRAYER FOR INFLAMMATION / STENOSIS OF THE SPINE: *(Lay hands on the affected area of the spine if known.)*

Father, inflammation has triggered arthritis in the joints of this spine. In the name of Jesus, I speak to these abnormal changes which are causing chronic back pain and stiffness. Inflammation, you have to leave. Any bone deposits interfering with

normal communication between the brain and the body have to leave in Jesus' name. Any damage caused by these changes is healed and is gone. Amen.

Fractures

Fractures of any part of the spine can cause serious issues such as compression of the nerves leading to permanent damage/paralysis of an area of the body. A fracture or break in a bone can be caused by trauma, sudden severe stress or twisting, weakening of the bone (osteoporosis), or tumors (cancer). It can be life threatening and requires immediate medical attention.

PRAYER FOR FRACTURES OF THE SPINE: *(Lay hands on the affected area as you pray.)*

Father, a bone in this spine has weakened, broken, and is now interfering with the communication between the brain and the body. I speak total healing to the bone. The fracture will heal without any scar tissue or abnormal strength. Any possible osteoporosis or other cause must leave in Jesus' name. Any damage caused by this fracture is healed and back to normal function in Jesus' name. Spirit of trauma, you have to leave now in Jesus' name. Memories of this event have to leave. Amen.

Sacroiliac joint pain

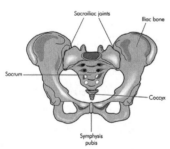

Sacroiliac joint pain or SI joint pain originates in the area where the sacrum and iliac bones meet. If you recall, the sacrum is the triangular shaped bone in the lower end of the spine. The iliac bones are the two large bones of the pelvis. The sacrum and iliac bones are held together by strong ligaments. Supporting the entire weight of the upper body, these joints endure a large amount of stress which wears away the cartilage. Arthritis is the result.

Added stress and abnormal gait during pregnancy can also cause damage to this cartilage. Hormones released by the female pregnant body allow the ligaments to relax in preparation for childbirth. This increase in stress can cause a joint dysfunction.

Any abnormal walking pattern places increased stress on the SI joints. This includes one leg longer than the other, or pain in any area of the hip, knee, ankle, or foot. Severe pain in a lower extremity often indicates there is a problem in either the lower back (lumbar spine) or SI joints. Often, if the underlying problem is treated, the associated back or SI joint dysfunction will also improve.

There are many disorders that can also cause inflammation in the SI joints including gout, rheumatoid arthritis, psoriasis, and ankylosing spondylitis. These are all forms of arthritis that can affect all joints. Ankylosing spondylitis is an inflammatory arthritis that always affects the SI joints. It can lead to chronic stiffness and severe pain. Ankylosing is another way of saying fusion – no further movement is possible. Once fusion occurs, the pain associated with the SI joints will be gone.

PRAYER FOR SI JOINT PROBLEMS: *(Place your hand on the lower back / or both hips.)*

I speak new cartilage to the SI joints in this body. Any inflammation is gone, arthritic or gouty changes are dissolved, and any problem with the back is removed. Mobility of the joint is restored.

If the person is a female who recently had a baby, add... *Pelvis, return to proper position. Hormones go back to normal levels and ligaments tighten up to usual strength and support.*

Check length of both legs. If one leg is shorter than the other, add... *Ligaments, muscles, and tendons, relax into proper alignment so both legs are even in length in Jesus' name. Amen.*

Rotator Cuff Injury

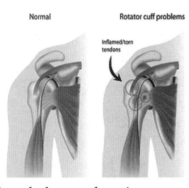

Normal   Rotator cuff problems

Inflamed/torn tendons

A common shoulder problem is called a rotator cuff injury which can be either a sprain or tear. The "cuff" is made up of several very strong ligaments which control the multiple movements of the shoulder. Injury can severely restrict movement of the upper arm. Lifting, pushing, pulling, balance, dressing, carrying objects, driving—so many activities of daily living are seriously affected by a rotator cuff problem. It is often an injury of athletes; however, everyone is vulnerable.

Damaged Meniscus

Another common sports injury is a damaged meniscus. This special protective padding is located within the knee. It is usually torn by abnormal movement of the knee joint. If severe enough, surgical repair is necessary.

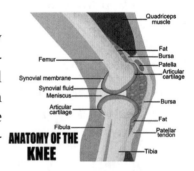

Quadriceps muscle
Fat
Bursa
Femur
Patella
Articular cartilage
Synovial membrane
Synovial fluid
Meniscus
Articular cartilage
Bursa
Fat
Fibula
Patellar tendon
ANATOMY OF THE KNEE
Tibia

PRAYER FOR SHOULDER ROTATOR CUFF OR TORN MENISCUS OF THE KNEE: *(Lay your hand on the involved part of the body.)*

Father, I speak to this injured body part (name the rotator cuff or knee). Pain, you have to leave. I curse any trauma related

to this injury and any inflammation in this area. Any damaged tissue is healed and back to normal strength and flexibility. Mobility is restored in Jesus' name. Amen.

Arthritis of Bone, Damage to Joints

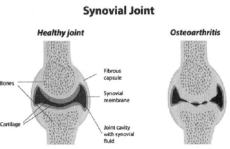

Synovial Joint

When arthritis or bone damage is severely debilitating to the movement of a joint, replacement is the usual medical recommendation. The most common joints replaced are the hips and knees; however, shoulders are also done. With severe rheumatoid arthritis, finger joints can also be replaced.

PRAYER FOR ARTHRITIS / BONE DAMAGE: *(Lay your hand near the affected part of the body.)*

I curse the trauma and the pain caused by this injury. I speak a new part into this body in Jesus' name.

PRAYER FOR A SURGICALLY REPLACED BODY JOINT *(Lay your hand near the affected part of the body.)*

Father, we give thanks for the talented surgeons who do so much to help us live healthy and productive lives. They have surgically replaced a damaged joint in this body. I speak to this joint to return to normal mobility, strength, and flexibility. Pain is gone in Jesus' name. I curse all scar tissue left from surgery. It is gone in Jesus' name.

In case the prosthesis (artificial joint) is causing the issue, you can add: *I speak a complete new replacement joint into this knee (or shoulder or hip). Normal function, return in Jesus' name.*

After praying for someone with a back injury or condition, differentiate between lingering soreness or stiffness and pain.

The pain and what caused it should be gone, but people may have to work out soreness or stiffness in the muscles or joints that have not been in use over a long period of time. Holy Ghost Therapy might be needed. Encourage them to move the affected area as they repeat, "Thank You, Jesus!"

Muscles need to be exercised regularly to regain strength and elasticity. Start with easy movements of the affected area and slowly increase until normal function is realized. Remember, "If you don't use it, you lose it." To strengthen any area of the remarkable body God created for each of us, it must be used. It must be exercised.

Testimony:
Doctor Roy and
Norma Jean Leroy

During the years of the Healing Explosions, much of what we learned about the spine came from the teachings of Dr. Roy Leroy, an accomplished and very successful chiropractor. His wife, Norma Jean, became involved with Hunter Ministries after she received a miraculous healing of her back.

Many years ago, Norma Jean was seriously injured in a devastating automobile accident. Following numerous surgeries and back fusions, she was basically wheelchair bound when she met Charles and Frances Hunter. Following prayer, Norma Jean was totally healed. Even though x-rays showed the hardware which fused her spine, she could bend and twist like a normal person after receiving her healing.

After meeting and marrying Dr. LeRoy, they ministered healing around the country as "Impossible Miracles Ministry". They attended all the Healing Explosions and contributed greatly to the Doctor's Panels as well as ministering to the sick. Norma Jean's testimony always inspired faith in others to believe and receive true healing from the Master. We appreciate and thank Dr. Roy and Norma Jean LeRoy for their faithful contributions.

CIRCULATION ISSUES:

Aneurysms

An aneurysm is an abnormal bulging or defect in the wall of an artery. There are three layers of tissue in the wall of a blood vessel. As this "ballooning" occurs in the defective artery, the two inner layers rupture or tear while the outer layer "bulges" outward. The constant pressure exerted by the blood being pumped through the body can cause an increase in the damaged area until it literally bursts.

The most common and most serious aneurysm occurs in the aorta, the largest artery of the body which carries the blood from the heart to the rest of the body. When an aortic aneurysm ruptures, the person usually dies very quickly. An aneurysm in the brain can also be fatal; however, depending on its location, it can also leave the same long-term effects of a stroke, e.g., paralysis, problems swallowing and talking, or dementia. Aneurysms can occur in any artery directly affected by high blood pressure or hypertension; however, other arteries rarely burst and, if they do, the results are rarely life threatening. Control of blood pressure is important in prevention and treatment of all types of aneurysms.

PRAYER FOR ANEURYSMS: *(Lay your hand on the approximate area of the diagnosed aneurysm.)*

Father, the blood vessels in this body have weakened walls and have developed abnormal pockets. I curse the trauma and effects of stress on this body. I speak new blood vessels with healthy strong walls into this body in Jesus' name. I speak to any high blood pressure causing this abnormal condition. Blood pressure, go back to normal. Any damage throughout the body caused by this high blood pressure, be healed and return to normal function. Amen.

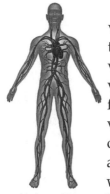

Varicose Veins

Blood returns to the heart through the veins of the body. The muscles of the legs help to pump the blood upward along with small valves within the veins. Varicose veins can develop when the veins weaken, the valves malfunction, or the return flow is blocked. The veins slowly but surely enlarge until they bulge outward at skin level. Usually purple from an abnormal collection of stagnant blood blocked within, the swollen, twisted vessels of the lower legs are often painful. Contributing factors can include standing or sitting for extended periods of time, wearing constricting clothing (e.g., girdles or tight nylons held up with rubber bands), overweight abdomens, or pregnancy.

Hemmorrhoids

Hemorrhoids are also a form of varicose veins. The blood circulation around the rectum is blocked for a prolonged period of time causing an enlargement of these blood vessels. The most common contributing factor is chronic constipation. The continuous weight of carrying a baby during pregnancy is often a cause in women. The external form of hemorrhoids is easily identified because they protrude outside of the rectum. Internal hemorrhoids are contained within the colon. Both types can be very painful. The fragile nature of the mucous membrane tissue and blood vessels of this area can easily be irritated by frequent bowel movements. Rectal bleeding can indicate a blood vessel has ruptured either inside or outside. Since passing blood with stool can also be a symptom of colon cancer or serious internal bleeding, medical evaluation is important to determine the actual cause. Obtaining a medical diagnosis also helps with more specific prayers for healing.

PRAYER FOR HEMORRHOIDS: *(Lay your hand on the lower back.)*

Father, these abnormal changes within these blood vessels are painful. I curse any trauma and effects of stress on this body. I speak healing to all the damaged blood vessels in this body. The valves and walls of the arteries will strengthen and function normally. Any damage is healed. Pain is gone in Jesus' name. Amen.

Pelvic Trauma

Pelvic trauma is usually the result of rape and can be experienced by both men and women. Cellular memory is very strong and can cause serious reactions years after the abuse occurred. This form of trauma can rear its ugly head years later and can seriously affect marital intimacy of any kind. Often, these events can be so repressed; a person has no memory of the initial event.

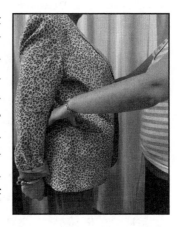

PRAYER FOR PELVIC TRAUMA. *(Have the person place their hand on their pelvic bones. You place your hand on top of theirs.)*

I speak to the trauma this person has experienced. I curse the trauma and effects of stress on this body. Trauma, you have to

leave in Jesus' name. Cellular memory, you will remember these
events no more. Body, you will function normally and never
recall any of the negative things that happened in the past.
Healthy intimacy will not only be possible, but will improve in
their relationship with their spouse in Jesus' name. Amen.

Lyme Disease

Lyme disease is caused by a bacteria spread by ticks. It is
not passed from person to person. Initially, its characteristic ex-
panding rings of redness at the site of the bite is described as
a "target". As it progresses, this unpleasant disease can cause
abnormalities of the skin, joints, heart, and nervous system.

The redness of the skin can be accompanied by generalized fatigue, muscle and joint stiffness, swollen glands, and
headache, resembling symptoms of a virus infection. The redness around the bite may resolve in a few weeks; however,
the bacteria continues to spread throughout the body causing
problems with other body systems. Inflammation of the heart
muscle can result in abnormal heart rhythms and heart failure.
When the nervous system is affected, facial muscle paralysis
(Bell's palsy), abnormal sensation due to disease of peripheral
nerves (peripheral neuropathy), meningitis, and confusion can
develop. Arthritis, or inflammation in the joints, begins with
swelling, stiffness, and pain. This arthritis which usually affects the knees can appear to be inflammatory arthritis and can
become chronic. Anxiety and depression both occur with an
increased rate in people infected with Lyme disease.

PRAYER FOR LYME DISEASE: *(Connect with the person*
you are praying for. Since the symptoms or problems can ap-
pear in many areas of the body, lay hands on the part with the
most serious symptoms as you pray.)

Father, this body is filled with Jesus' Spirit. Bacteria, you can-
not live in this body. I speak death to every bacteria that has

attacked this body. I speak life to every cell in this body. Any damage to the heart, skin, nerves, or joints caused by this attack is now healed completely in Jesus' name. This body is normal and whole from the top of their head to the bottom of their feet in Jesus' name.

West Nile Virus

The mosquito spreads the West Nile Virus infection. If you are bitten by a mosquito carrying this virus, your symptoms may be minor; however, some people who become infected with West Nile virus develop a life-threatening illness that includes inflammation of the brain, called encephalitis.

About 20 percent of people develop a mild infection called West Nile fever. Common signs and symptoms of West Nile fever include: fever, headache, body aches, fatigue, skin rash, swollen lymph glands, or eye pain.

In a small percentage of infected people, the virus causes a serious neurological infection. This may include inflammation of the brain (encephalitis) and/or surrounding membranes (meningoencephalitis). Serious infection may also include infection and inflammation of the membranes surrounding the brain and spinal cord (meningitis), inflammation of the spinal cord (West Nile poliomyelitis), and acute flaccid paralysis — a sudden weakness in your arms, legs or breathing muscles.

Signs and symptoms of these more serious diseases include: High fever, severe headache, stiff neck, disorientation or confusion, stupor or coma, tremors or muscle jerking, lack of coordination, convulsions, pain, partial paralysis, or sudden serious weakness. Diagnosis must be made by a doctor.

Signs and symptoms of West Nile fever usually last a few days, but sign and symptoms of encephalitis or meningitis can linger for weeks, and certain neurological effects, such as muscle weakness, may be permanent. Hospitalization is generally required for encephalitis or meningitis.

PRAYER FOR WEST NILE VIRUS: *(Lay your hand on the forehead/head and or upper chest while you pray the following prayer.)*

Virus and bacteria in this body, I curse you in Jesus' name. Every cell of abnormal infection in this body has to go now. Any damage caused by this inflammation or infection is healed in Jesus' name. There is no more confusion, abnormal movement of body parts, paralysis or weakness in this body. Immune system, you are strong and fighting off all the negative effects of these bugs that have attacked this body. This body is normal and whole right now. Thank You, Jesus.

Lymph System

The lymph system is made up of lymph nodes, lymph ducts, and lymph vessels that both produce and transport lymph from tissues to the bloodstream. The lymph system is a vital part of the body's immune system. The lymph nodes produce immune cells that aid the immune system in removing and destroying waste, foreign material, debris, dead blood cells, pathogens, toxins, and cancer cells.

Lymph fluid is made of white blood cells called lymphocytes, the cells that attack bacteria in the blood and fluid from the intestines. The lymphatic system absorbs fats and fat-soluble vitamins from the digestive system and delivers these nutrients to the cells of the body where they are used by the cells. It also transports the white blood cells from the bones (where they are created) to the blood circulation. Lymph fluid is plasma released from blood in the tiny blood vessels throughout the body. Once it has done its job of filtering debris, the fluid returns upward to the neck where it returns to the blood circulation.

Lymph nodes are soft, small pockets which usually cannot be seen or easily felt. They are located in various parts of the body, such as the neck, armpit, groin, and inside the center of the chest and abdomen. The most common lymph nodes are the tonsils, adenoids, spleen, and thymus. When bacteria are recognized in the lymph fluid during the filtration process, the lymph nodes produce more infection-fighting white blood cells. This increase in fluid causes the nodes to swell and can cause pain.

Lymphedema

Lymphedema can develop in either the arms or legs when a blockage occurs in the lymphatic drainage system. If lymph nodes are surgically removed during a mastectomy, lymph fluid is trapped in the arm causing an extremely large upper extremity. The arm and hand can be so large that its function is severely impaired. A blockage in the lower extremities causes extreme swelling (edema) in both legs causing serious functional impairment to walking, moving, and dressing. Lymphedema of the legs is often related to cancer treatment radiation which destroys the lymph system along with the malignant tissues.

The most extreme stage of this unpleasant disease is called elephantiasis. This massive swelling can occur anywhere in the body. The affected areas appear like elephant hide – hard, rough, and tight, with numerous folds and indentations, often discolored. The skin is very fragile and can break down very easily and heals with great difficulty.

PRAYER FOR ABNORMAL EDEMA OR SWELLING IN THE BODY: *(Place your hands on the affected area of the body.)*

I curse all abnormal collection of fluid in this body. I speak to all the lymph system to work properly and to drain all excess fluid out of this body in Jesus' name. Any abnormal function has to go now, leaving healthy tissue and normal function to

all damaged tissues. All excess stretched tissues and skin, re-turn to normal strength and elasticity in Jesus' name. Amen.

Hodgkin's Disease/Lymphoma

Hodgkin's disease is a type of cancer of the blood known as lymphoma. This type of cancer develops when white blood cells in the body becoming diseased or damaged and presents as a solid tumor of lymphoid cells. There are 35 types of lymphoma which can easily spread through the lymph system to other areas of the body.

PRAYER FOR HODGKIN'S DISEASE: *(Lay your hands near the affected part of the body.)*

I curse all cancerous cells present in this body. I curse all trauma and any negative effects of stress in this body. I speak brand new organs/tissues to replace every damaged cell. I speak to all abnormal function caused by this unnatural growth of lymph tissue. Be gone in Jesus' name. All damage to body tissue and/or circulation has to disappear and be replaced with healthy tissue, in Jesus' name.

Addison's Disease

Addison's disease is an endocrine or hormonal disorder characterized by weight loss, muscle weakness, fatigue, low blood pressure, and sometimes darkening of the skin. This disease occurs when the adrenal glands do not produce enough of the hormone cortisol and aldosterone. The disease is also called adrenal insufficiency.

Cortisol is produced by the adrenal glands, located just above the kidneys. Cortisol's most important job is to help the body respond to stress. Cortisol helps maintain blood pressure and heart function, helps slow the immune system's inflammation response, helps balance the effects of insulin in breaking down sugar for energy, helps regulate the metabolism of proteins, carbohydrates, and fats, and helps maintain proper arousal and sense of well-being.

PRAYER FOR ADDISON'S DISEASE *(Place your hands on each side of the person near the kidneys.)*

Father, the adrenal glands in this body are not functioning properly. I curse any trauma that has affected these small but important glands. I speak new adrenal glands into this body now in Jesus' name. Regulation of necessary hormones is normal. Any damage from this condition is gone in Jesus' name.

Autoimmune Diseases:

(Stress and Trauma always have effects on the immune system.)

The body's immune system fights against foreign bodies or dangerous substances which invade our bodies. Bacteria, parasites, cancer cells, and even transplanted organs and tissues can all trigger a response from the normal immune system which protects us from potential harmful things entering our bodies. Without a strong immune system, a body can be attacked by any and every bacteria. These foreign objects would cause serious diseases and inevitable death to a person. Animals in general all have specific immune systems which fight off what we commonly call infections.

When an immune system is compromised, a person can "catch" all types of infectious diseases. To protect this person from possible lethal bacteria, they will be put into isolation. One of the most well-known cases was "The Boy in the Bubble". The young man had to live in a sterile plastic bubble with no human contact or he would die. Everything he touched had to be meticulously cleaned including the air he breathed, the food he ate, and the water he drank.

Our body has a wonderfully intricate immune system which stays strong and ready to fight 24/7 as long as it has the correct nutrients, vitamins, and basic nutrition available. A healthy immune system fights off all the bad stuff we all come in contact with on a daily basis. Poor immunity means illness will be a frequent visitor.

There is a growing list of diseases which are considered "auto-immune" illnesses. This means the body's immune system doesn't correctly differentiate between foreign objects from normal body tissues. The "fighting" component of the immune system kicks in and attacks the body inappropriately. To attempt to stop this immune reaction, medications are given to slow or stop the inflammation. Usually, steroids are given. A person is now prone to catch anything that passes by because the immune system is weakened by the medication. When actual "bad" bacteria come by, the body can't stop it from causing a true infection.

Rheumatoid Arthritis

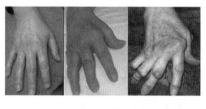

Rheumatoid Arthritis affects joints, lungs, nerves, skin and heart tissue. It can cause fatigue, joint pain and stiffness, deformed joints, shortness of breath, loss of sensation, rashes, chest pain, weakness, calcium bone deposits. (For prayer, see section under Bones, Rheumatoid Arthritis.)

Graves' Disease

Graves' Disease (Hyperthyroidism) – When there is too much hormone produced by the thyroid, there is a serious rise in the body's metabolism resulting in a sudden weight loss, a rapid or irregular heartbeat (often described as palpitations), excessive sweating, irritability, and nervousness.

PRAYER FOR GRAVES' DISEASE: *(Lay your hand on the area of the throat.)*

This gland is not functioning normally. I curse any trauma or side effects of stress that may be triggering the release of excess levels of the thyroid hormone. Any damage to other areas of the body caused by this abnormal activity, be healed in Jesus' name. Body, you will function normally like God intended and the immune system will come into alignment with proper levels of hormones from all areas of the body in Jesus' name.

Sjögren's Syndrome

Sjögren's syndrome – glands fail to produce the necessary moisture for mucous membranes in the mouth, nose, eyes, throat, and occasionally, the lungs. Without proper moisture, mucous membranes cannot maintain their integrity or stay healthy.

PRAYER FOR SJOGREN'S:

I curse the trauma and side effects of stress that have attacked this body. All symptoms have to go in Jesus' name. I speak healing to all the mucous membranes within this body. Mucous membranes are going to function normally and produce the moisture necessary for healthy, normal function in Jesus' name. Immune system, you will react normally to protect this body from outside substances and not attack the body's normal tissues.

Scleroderma

Progressive systemic sclerosis (also known as Scleroderma) is an overproduction of collagen under the skin. As the skin hardens, function is hindered. There is no cure; the "hardness" spreads through the body and into vital organs.

PRAYER FOR SCLERODERMA:

I curse the trauma and side effects of stress in this body. Collagen levels in this body will return to normal in Jesus' name. Normal function will return to the skin and all its layers. Any damage this disease has caused in other organs of the body will be healed and disappear in Jesus' name. Autoimmune reactions are gone in Jesus' name.

Glomerulonephritis

Glomerulonephritis is an inflammation or damage to the area of the kidneys that filter waste and fluids from the blood. It can lead to chronic kidney disease and/or kidney failure which require dialysis to maintain life.

PRAYER FOR GLOMERULONEPHRITIS: (Lay hands on lower edges of ribs at waist levels.)

I speak to all inflammation in these kidneys. All inflammation has to go in Jesus' name. Kidney function will return to normal with all filtration of impurities and fluid to work properly from this moment onward. All kidney disease or failure is gone in Jesus' name. No dialysis, no late effects of stress, no kidney transplant. In Jesus' name.

Lupus Erythematosus

Lupus erythematosus affects joints, kidneys, skin, lungs, heart, brain, and blood cells. Joints do not become deformed like rheumatoid arthritis; however, they do become inflamed and very painful.

PRAYER FOR LUPUS

Father, this autoimmune response is not of You. I curse trauma and any side effects of stress that have triggered this abnormal response from this body's immune system. All body systems

and organs will work and respond normally in Jesus' name. Any damage done to various areas of the body is gone. Pain is gone. Deformities are gone. Inflammation is gone. Lupus is totally gone in Jesus' name.

Diabetes Mellitus

Diabetes Mellitus means a destruction of cells of the pancreas which produce insulin to metabolize sugar into usable glucose for circulation throughout the body. Insulin injections are often required for life once the pancreas doesn't produce any insulin.

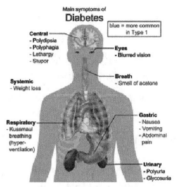

If uncontrolled, excess sugar circulates through the body damaging numerous organs and their function. For instance, a common complication is known as neuropathy, a decreased sensation of the fingers, hands, toes, and feet accompanied by shooting pains. Eventually, numbness can prevent communication between the affected tissue and the brain. A diabetic foot can have sores, injuries, ingrown nails, or gangrene without any pain to alert the person to serious complications of the feet. This can lead to amputations of toes, feet, and legs.

Changes to the eyes cause Diabetic Retinopathy which contributes to blindness. The numbness can extend to the heart tissue. A heart attack can occur without pain. The person won't seek medical assistance and may die from the heart damage. Injury to the kidneys leads to chronic kidney disease, renal insufficiency, and end-stage renal disease requiring regular dialysis treatments to maintain life.

Diabetes increases the risk for any type of medical procedure. It slows the body's regenerative ability. Healing of any tissue occurs slowly. Open wounds on the skin leave the body more susceptible to infection and inflammation. Erratic uncontrolled blood sugars can send a person into a diabetic coma or crisis very easily – either end of the spectrum can precipitate death.

PRAYER FOR DIABETES:

I curse the trauma and high stress that have overworked the endocrine glands of this pancreas. I speak a new pancreas into this body. Correct levels of insulin will be released by the new pancreas to metabolize the sugars necessary for the body to function at optimum levels. Any damage to any other area of the body is healed and like brand new in Jesus' name including the heart, the feet, the hands, the kidneys, and the nerves. All areas of the body are functioning normally in Jesus' name. Amen.

Anemia

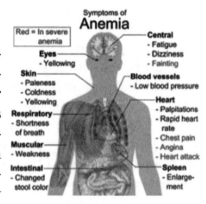

Anemia means the hemoglobin level of the blood is below normal levels. Oxygen necessary for life is transported from the lungs to the body cells by the hemoglobin within red blood cells. It can be caused by bleeding or hemorrhage, or by a lack of necessary nutrients in a diet. Without enough oxygen circulating through a body, the organs close down one by one until death occurs.

Hemolytic Anemia – the abnormal breakdown of red blood cells can be short or long term. One of the most commonly recognized diagnosis in this category is "sickle-cell anemia".

Pernicious Anemia – cells of the stomach lining can't absorb Vitamin B12 necessary to produce blood cells and maintain nerve cells.

PRAYER FOR ANEMIA:

I curse any trauma or effects of stress that have attacked this body. Any damage to healthy tissues that could possibly contribute to this anemia is gone in Jesus' name. This body will accept nutrients without a problem and produce enough healthy red blood cells to carry oxygen to all the cells of this body. Hemoglobin levels are normal. All blood circulation will function normally in Jesus' name.

Autoimmune Skin Issues

Bullous Pemphigoid is a disease characterized by skin blisters which can develop on any area of the skin. They can reappear again and again; usually affecting those over 64 years of age.

Pemphigus includes blisters on the skin or mucous membranes that can develop into sores which can be easily infected. If they affect the lungs, the changes are permanent and can be life threatening.

PRAYER FOR SKIN ISSUES:

Father, the skin makes up the largest organ of the human body and is vital to keeping us healthy. I curse any trauma to the skin. I curse any effects of stress that have attacked this skin. Any irritation or malfunction of the skin and all its layers must be restored to normal healthy levels in Jesus' name. Any damage that extends to the internal mucous membranes is gone. Any infection that has attached itself to this damaged tissue is destroyed and gone in Jesus' name.

Autoimmune Nerve Problems

Multiple Sclerosis. The protective covering of the nerves is damaged. Cells can't conduct nerve signals to communicate from the brain to the body. Symptoms include weakness,

abnormal sensations, vertigo, vision issues, muscle spasms, loss of control of
muscles, and incontinence.

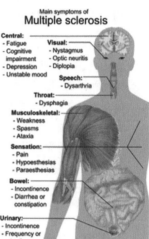

Main symptoms of
Multiple sclerosis

Central:
- Fatigue
- Cognitive impairment
- Depression
- Unstable mood

Visual:
- Nystagmus
- Optic neuritis
- Diplopia

Speech:
- Dysarthria

Throat:
- Dysphagia

Musculoskeletal:
- Weakness
- Spasms
- Ataxia

Sensation:
- Pain
- Hypoesthesias
- Paraesthesias

Bowel:
- Incontinence
- Diarrhea or constipation

Urinary:
- Incontinence
- Frequency or retention

Myasthenia gravis. Muscles don't
receive the instructions from the brain
due to blockage of communication at the
neuromuscular junction.

PRAYER FOR PROBLEMS
WITH NERVE COMMUNICATION:

*I curse whatever is causing the inter-
ruption in communication between the
brain and the rest of this body. Father, I speak a whole new
nervous system into this body so it will function and respond
with normal communication from this day forward in Jesus'
name. Sensations, instructions, and responses will flow freely
and appropriately from the brain through the spinal cord and
out to the nerves controlling life. All prions are gone in Jesus'
name.*

Autoimmune GI Diseases...

Crohn's disease is an autoimmune inflammatory bowel disease that usually affects the intestines, but can cause problems
from the mouth to the rectum. The most common symptoms include uncontrollable diarrhea, abdominal pain, and weight loss.
Some call it an autoimmune disease while others simply call it
an immune deficiency. Regardless of what causes it, a person
with this disease knows where every bathroom is located and
plans activities within a few minutes from this necessary room.

Medical research list predisposing factors as: genetic mark-
ers, family history, environmental factors, body's over-reaction
to normal bacteria in the intestines, being Jewish and/or smoking. It usually occurs in people between ages 15 - 35. The more

serious cases often result in surgical removal of the severely damaged bowel resulting in an ileostomy or colostomy (intestine is connected to the outside abdominal wall where stool is collected in a plastic bag).

Since we have learned about stress and trauma, we are adding to the medical findings.

PRAYER FOR CROHN'S DISEASE: *(Lay a hand on the person's abdomen.)*

I curse the spirit of trauma and effects of stress that have attached to this body. Abnormal bowel function has to leave. I speak normal digestion to every inch of the GI (gastrointestinal) tract. No more diarrhea, no more constipation, no more abdominal pains, no more stomach meds, no more surgery looming in the future, and no more embarrassment. Body function will be normal from this day forward in Jesus' name. Amen.

If surgical intervention is imminent or planned in the future, add: *I speak a whole new intestinal tract into this body in Jesus' name.*

Closely related to the symptoms of Crohn's disease is **IBS**, or **Irritable Bowel Syndrome**. Aggravated by stress, the bowel moves the waste material through the intestinal system rapidly resulting in frequent unexpected diarrhea episodes.

Years ago, the terms "heartburn" or "indigestion" were often used to describe an unpleasant burning sensation of the esophagus often accompanied with burping or belching. The valve between the esophagus and stomach would open and allow the food being processed in the stomach to back up toward the mouth. The burning feeling is caused by the digestive juices released into the stomach to breakdown food into usable form for the body to absorb and utilize. A more common term, Acid Reflux, is used today.

Excess acid in the stomach, usually from stress, irritates the lining of the stomach and may cause a stomach ulcer (open wound). If the ulcer eats through the stomach wall and pours the acid contents of the stomach into the belly, this life-threatening situation requires immediate medical attention. The acid which is so normal within the stomach will start digesting other tissues while the blood from the wound will drop the hemoglobin layers not to mention the severe pain a person will experience.

PRAYER FOR ABNORMAL BOWEL FUNCTION: (Lay your hand on the abdomen. Men, ask person to lay their hand on their abdomen first, then lay your hand on their hand.)

I curse whatever has caused this intestinal dysfunction. I speak a new intestine into this body. Crohn's disease and IBS, you have to leave this person in Jesus' name. Any residual damage or malfunction must be replaced by whole, new tissue that will accept normal everyday food without all the indigestion, belching, and discolored stools that occurred previously. (Name)_____ can enjoy normal food again in Jesus' name.

Sleep Disorder

Insomnia is a common condition in which a person has trouble falling asleep at night or staying asleep. Many things can contribute to this sleep disorder including anxiety, stress, depression, pain, respiratory difficulties, jet lag, caffeine, medications with stimulant components, abnormal environment (loud noises e.g., snoring or unpleasant temperatures).

PRAYER FOR INSOMNIA: *(Lay hands on shoulders or head.)*

I curse the insomnia that has been causing sleepless nights for this body and mind. I curse any trauma and side effects of stress that has contributed to the insomnia. I speak the mela-

tonin levels be normal and allow a normal peaceful 8 hours of sleep every night in Jesus' name.

MYALGIAS
Fibromyalgia / Chronic Fatigue Syundrome

Both of these diagnoses actually comprise a group of vague symptoms with no identified cause. Unexplainable aches and pains in various areas of the body, tender sensitive points at certain joints, tiredness with no exertion, and other general complaints have been thrown into this category. Several years ago, they were classified in the psychological realm; they are now considered a medical diagnosis and often treated with something other than psych medications. Diagnosis is made only after ruling out all the other diagnoses that have similar symptoms. With no definitive tests to prove or disprove the person's complaints, the diagnosis is made on the combination of many vague complaints. Often, history will show some form of excessive stress within months before the onset.

PRAYER FOR FIBROMYALGIA / CHRONIC FATIGUE SYNDROME:

I curse the trauma and side effects of stress that have affected this body. Pain and tiredness of chronic fatique are gone in Jesus' name. I speak refreshing sleep every night, alert and energetic days to accomplish God's plan for this life, and an exciting encouraging creative life for years ahead. No more aches, pains, exhaustion, tiredness, insomnia, stress, worry, disability, helplessness, or mental "fog". I speak life to every cell of this body in Jesus' name.

ABOUT JOAN HUNTER

Joan Hunter is a compassionate minister, dynamic teacher, an accomplished author, and an anointed healing evangelist. She has devoted her life to carry the message of hope, deliverance, and healing to the nations. As president and founder of Joan Hunter Ministries, Hearts 4 Him, and 4 Corners Healing and Conference Center, her vision is to equip believers to take the healing power of God beyond the 4 walls of the church to the 4 corners of the earth.

Joan ministers the Gospel with manifestations of supernatural signs and wonders in healing encounters, healing schools, miracles, services, conference, churches, and revival centers around the world. She heads up the Worldwide Day of Healing that she and her parents started in 2005. Being sensitive to the move of the Spirit, Joan speaks prophetically in the services corporately as well as releasing personal prophetic ministry to those in attendance. Joan's genuine approach and candid delivery enables her to connect intimately with people from all educational, social, and cultural backgrounds. Some have described her as having a Carol Burnett sense of humor with the anointing of Jesus.

Joan Hunter brings a powerful ministry to a world characterized by brokenness and pain. Having emerged victorious through tragic circumstances, impossible obstacles, and immeasurable devastation, Joan is able to share a message of hope and restoration to the brokenhearted, deliverance and freedom to the bound, and healing and wholeness to the diseased. Joan's life is one of uncompromising dedication to the Gospel of Jesus Christ, and she exhibits a sincere desire to see the Body of Christ live free, happy, and whole.

Joan committed her life to Christ at the tender age of 12 and began faithfully serving in His Kingdom. She has served in ministry alongside her parents, Charles and Frances Hunter, as they traveled around the globe ministering in healing schools, miracle services, and healing explosions. Prior to branching out into her own international healing ministry, Joan co-pastored a church for 18 years.

Joan has authored 13 books; *Healing the Whole Man Handbook, Healing the Heart, Power to Heal, Freedom Beyond Comprehension, Healing Miracles and Supernatural Experiences, How to Receive and Minister the Baptism of the Holy Spirit, Healing Starts Now, Supernatural Provision, Covering the Basics, How to Receive and Maintain Your Healing, Powerful Encounters in the God Realm (with Patricia King), Like a Diamond, Journal of Miracles.*

Joan has ministered in miracle services and conducted healing school in numerous countries, including: the United States, Haiti, El Salvador, Hong King, New Zealand, the Republic of the Philippines, Brazil, Colombia, Guatemala, Australia, Canada, Northern Ireland, Ireland, Israel, England, Mexico, Peru, Singapore, Japan, Belgium, Russia, Panama, and the Ukraine. She has also had numerous television and radio appearances, including Sid Roth's "It's Supernatural", "It's a New Day", "The Miracle Channel", Steve Shultz's "Prophetic TV", and many others. Joan's television appearances have been broadcast around the world on World Harvest Network, Inspiration Network, Daystar, Faith TV, Cornerstone TV, The Church Channel, Extreme Prophetic with Patricia King, Total Christian Television, Christian Television Network, Watchman Broadcasting, Today with Marilyn (Hickey) and Sara, and GOD TV.

Joan and her husband, Kelley Murrell, reside in Pinehurst, Texas (NW Houston). They have four daughters, four sons, and six grandchildren.

BOOKING INFORMATION
Phone 281-789-7500
Email: info@joanhunter.org
www.joanhunter.org

Benefits of Membership in the 4 Corners Alliance...

An alliance is an agreement, coalition, or friendship between two or more parties, made in order to advance common goals and to secure common interests. It is also a political agreement between countries to support each other in disputes with other countries.

To be an "ally" is to unite formally, as by treaty, league, marriage; to associate or connect by some mutual relationship or friendship; to enter into an alliance; join; or unite. It is a person, group, or nation that is associated with another or others for some common cause, purpose or support.

There is always strength in numbers. When going through life's challenges, sharing with and praying with another always helps ease the bumps or scrapes along the path to victory. God made us for relationship. We share, talk, feel, care about, love, correct, assist, encourage, as well as pray for one another. None of us would survive long without other people and what they can contribute to our lives.

Hopefully, you and your ministry will have spiritual support from your local church, however, you may find you are the only one in your world who believes healing is for today and that miracles are an everyday occurrence. Occasionally, a church may frown and request you find another church home.

Maybe you have a spouse or family member to encourage you; however, they too may not wholeheartedly agree with your spiritual choice.

Instead of walking down a lonely road feeling isolated and confused, you want to align yourself with people who will support you and pray for you on a regular basis. Where do you find someone to answer questions and support you on your new journey into ministry?

Agreement

Whoever you come into alliance with, make sure you agree with their beliefs and teachings. Examine the fruit of the ministry. Are they doing things you want to do? Are they staying updated on what God is saying today or are they stuck in teachings of 50 years ago? Do they believe in the power and infilling of the Holy Spirit? Or do they scoff at words of knowledge or being slain in the Spirit?

Just like a man and woman can't walk into marriage without agreement, alignment with a ministry must also have agreement. When you join such an alliance and support their ministry, the anointing on the head of the ministry alliance flows downward onto all the members and supporting staff. To walk in agreement is totally scriptural. Even God believes there is strength in numbers.

Can two walk together, except they be agreed? (Amos 3:3 KJV)

Again I say unto you, That if two of you shall agree on earth as touching any thing that they shall ask, it shall be done for them of my Father which is in heaven (Matthew 18:19 KJV).

Five of you shall chase a hundred, and a hundred of you shall put ten thousand to flight; your enemies shall fall by the sword before you (Leviticus 26:8).

The focus of Joan Hunter Ministries is healing of all areas of life including body, mind, spirit, and finances. Do you want to share the fruit of Joan Hunter Ministries? Then join in agreement with the 4 Corners Alliance and share in our anointing. Remember, whatever ministry you support and work with, their anointing will also spread over you, your life, and your ministry.

Drawing on the Anointing and the Experience

Joan Hunter freely shares her experience and knowledge with others around the world. Whatever revelations Joan receives from God, she freely passes on to those searching for God's best. No secret anointing. No secret words. No hidden prayers. She is open and forthcoming with everything. It is your choice to learn from her experience rather than start at square one with what to do and what not to do. She has been there and done that, and can prevent you from fumbling or stumbling down the wrong path.

Opportunities for learning and drawing on Joan's anointing and experience are freely available through meetings held around the world, through her books, CD's and DVD's, and through the live streaming of her meetings online. Being connected by way of her website means you will know exactly what she is doing and where. Sign up for her emails and you will also receive her regular updates, prophecies, and new revelations as well as the release of her latest book(s), teaching materials, and ministry tools.

Joan's goal is to train and equip believers to travel, teach, and minister to the 4 corners of their world and then onward to the 4 corners of the earth. Millions are waiting to hear the Good News. She can't do it alone; however, multiplying herself through every alliance member makes a great dent in the need for willing and able ministers to spread the gospel and touch those millions of searching and hurting people.

Alignment is Credibility

The Bible teaches that in the last days people will follow strange winds of doctrine. A parent checks out their children's friends, school, and teachers to assure a safe environment is maintained. No parent wants a child to experience an unhealthy situation which could potentially cause harm. Any ministry leader will do the same.

That we should no longer be children, tossed to and fro and carried about with every wind of doctrine, by the trickery of men, in the cunning craftiness of deceitful plotting(Ephesians 4:14).

Now the Spirit expressly says that in latter times some will depart from the faith, giving heed to deceiving spirits and doctrines of demons (1 Timothy 4:1).

If you instruct the brethren in these things, you will be a good minister of Jesus Christ, nourished in the words of faith and of the good doctrine which you have carefully followed (1 Timothy 4:6).

Meditate on these things; give yourself entirely to them, that your progress may be evident to all. Take heed to yourself and to the doctrine. Continue in them, for in doing this you will save both yourself and those who hear you (1 Timothy 4:15-16).

Preach the word! Be ready in season and out of season. Convince, rebuke, exhort, with all longsuffering and teaching. For the time will come when they will not endure sound doctrine, but according to their own desires, because they have itching ears, they will heap up for themselves teachers; and they will turn their ears away from the truth, and be turned aside to fables (2 Timothy 4:2-4).

Starting out in ministry is a challenge. Who knows you? Who can give a reference? Who will substantiate what you stand for?

You have no reputation, no credibility without a legitimate and respected recommendation.

Realistically, some who were your associates or friends may not agree with your new beliefs and current revelations. You may have to give up some friends, but know that God has others waiting to welcome you. You have an exciting new path ahead of you. 4 Corner Alliance was designed to come alongside of you and help you stay on the path to successful ministry.

Realize also that the mandate to protect now covers you and those you minister to and associate with. You will gain a following, your sheep. You will now become their protector, their mentor. What you teach will be held under close scrutiny both from man and God.

Not many of you should become teachers, my fellow believers, because you know that we who teach will be judged more strictly (James 3:1 NIV).

Those truly chosen by God to teach others and minister to the needs of the Body of Christ, need to have a close relationship with the Father, Son, and Holy Spirit. That means communicating with Him, studying His Word, and serving others with humility and compassion. You will be held to a higher standard of godly living by the world as well as the church. However, with God at your side, you will have His constant advice and guidance.

Now therefore, go, and I will be with your mouth and teach you what you shall say (Exodus 4:12).

Commitment and Covering

Besides drawing on the experience of Joan Hunter Ministries, you will meet the other Alliance members and make lifelong connections. Sharing experiences with other leaders across the country will increase your anointing, knowledge, and ministry influence. Christian networking is powerful. You will meet many members during Joan's meetings and other gatherings. Praying for each other will strengthen your connections and friendships.

In addition, you will be provided with ministry opportunities. When Joan is ministering in your area, you will be contacted and invited to minister with her. Do you have a desire to minister out of the country? Join Joan in traveling to such places as Ireland or Haiti and you will share in and learn about ministering in a foreign country. Many phone requests for prayer come into the main office. If someone in your area desires a hospital visit, for example, the office may call you to meet that need.

You will join a big family that is increasing regularly. The ministry staff prays for all the Alliance membership regularly. In return, we ask the Alliance members as well as other partners to pray for the ministry as we travel and work for Him. Many testimonies have come in through the years from friends of the ministry sharing their victories, healings, financial breakthroughs, and miracles. Imagine the connection Alliance members have with the ministry! It is even stronger because of the agreement of the Alliance.

We welcome hearing about your victories and testimonies. Each miracle reported encourages everyone to keep on going. It confirms we are in God's perfect will as we follow Him and spread His Good News. Just as we encourage someone who was healed to testify about their miracle, we encourage those who minister to do the same thing. Knowing what God does through the one ministering is just as exciting, and you need to share those miracles with others. One miracle shared can multiply to many listeners who then have the faith for their miracle.

Questions

What do you do when you have a question about the ministry? Where do you go? Who do you contact? Who do you call? It may seem that there isn't anyone nearby with a correct answer, or should I say an experienced answer. Part of membership in the 4 Corners Alliance is an open-phone policy. You can call the 4 Corners Alliance during office hours and submit any question you have. You can also contact the Alliance through the Internet at 4ca@joanhunter.org.

Your question will be directed to the person best suited to give a proper answer. That means Joan may be answering the question if no one else is appropriate. The Alliance staff is committed to you…to help and assist you with advice whenever you have a need.

Power of Unity

Look again at the definition of "alliance." It is the "political agreement between countries to support each other in disputes with other countries." Joining the Alliance means you and your "world" (country) agree with the other Alliance members' "worlds" (countries) in fighting the enemy (satan). It is God's Truth against satan's lies (disputes).

We will stand together with common goals, doctrines, and beliefs founded on God's Word. We will fight the enemy by getting God's kids saved, healed, and made whole. We will not only add to the Army of God, we will multiply it until the earth is covered with His Power and Glory.

The benefits of membership will far outshine what little is described here. Join the 4 Corners Alliance.

Blessings!!!

Joan